THE COMPLETE GUIDE TO
Buying a Business

THE COMPLETE GUIDE TO
Buying a Business

Richard W. Snowden

American Management Association

New York • Atlanta • Boston • Chicago • Kansas City • San Francisco • Washington, D.C.
Brussels • Toronto • Mexico City • Tokyo

This book is available at a special
discount when ordered in bulk quantities.
For information, contact Special Sales Department,
AMACOM, a division of American Management Association,
135 West 50th Street, New York, NY 10020.

This publication is designed to provide accurate and authoritative information in regard to the subject matter covered. It is sold with the understanding that the publisher is not engaged in rendering legal, accounting, or other professional service. If legal advice or other expert assistance is required, the services of a competent professional person should be sought.

Library of Congress Cataloging-in-Publication Data

Snowden, Richard W.
    The complete guide to buying a business / Richard W. Snowden.
        p.   cm.
    Include bibliographical references and index.
    ISBN 0-8144-5158-6 :
    1. Small business—Purchasing—Handbooks, manuals, etc.
I. Title.
HD1393.25.S655   1993
658.1'6—dc20   93-27767
                                                       CIP

Printing number

10 9 8 7 6 5 4 3 2 1

To
Robin
who contributed so much to this book
and so much more to my life

Contents

Introduction

Finding and buying a business that provides both psychic and financial rewards is the dream of millions. Disillusioned with the corporate rat race, people much like you have decided to chuck it and seek fulfillment and financial security through owning their own businesses. For many, that has meant becoming self-employed or starting a new business. For others, it has meant buying a franchise or an existing small business.

If you fall into the latter category, this book is for you. Finding the *right* business and *buying it right* can be one of the greatest satisfactions of professional life. It can bring unparalleled personal fulfillment and financial reward. It can remove you from the politics and the insanities of corporate life. It can free you from the limitations of being a wage slave and guarantee you control of your own destiny.

Sadly, most people never find the right business, one that fits their skills and interests and is affordable, profitable, and secure. Those who eventually do buy a small business frequently find reality is quite different from what they had imagined. Long, grueling hours, financial pressures, employee problems, and unhappy customers take their toll. The pretty picture painted by the previous owner turns out to have been an illusion. All too often, financial ruin follows.

If you're just starting out on your quest to find and buy a business, it may surprise you to know that fully three-quarters of wannabee business owners fail to ever find a profitable, secure business that fits their skills and interests. That's the bad news. The good news is that if you know what you're doing, the odds of finding the business that's exactly right for you are really quite good.

Knowing what to do and doing it right the first time are what this book is all about. It's a hands-on manual designed to be used as a blueprint for the successful acquisition of a small business that fits your needs as well as your pocketbook. The emphasis is on how to accomplish your goal using a detailed action plan that is solidly grounded in the realities of your assets and liabilities and the experience of those who have successfully made the transition to the world of happy business ownership.

This is not a course in investment banking, accounting, or business law. It won't replace your lawyer or your accountant. You'll still need both. Neither is it a scheme for finding a business that will make you a fortune with no work. But the approach detailed here can work wonders. However, it will work only if you use it as directed.

It's astounding to see the number of people who are looking for a business with no idea of what's right for them. And even when their goal is clearly defined, most people have no idea where to look. Fewer still have any clue about how to evaluate a company's profit potential accurately, how to place a selling price on a potential acquisition, or how to negotiate a deal that pleases both buyer and seller.

Although this book answers these questions, it was written to provide more than answers. Finding and buying the business that's right for you is a *process*. You must first understand the process and then execute it if you are to realize your goal. The process of finding and buying a business as detailed in this book is based on the knowledge, skills, and actions of thousands of successful buyers. If you wish to avoid joining the vast majority of people who come up short in their search for the ideal business, you need only commit yourself to this proven road map.

If you're one of the many who've repeatedly failed to find your dream business, you may be surprised that a book like this can be so effective. However, if you make this self-directed process your priority and if you make the necessary effort, you'll not only find your business, you'll also enjoy unprecedented career fulfillment and economic success.

Acknowledgments

Although I was the recorder for this book, the content was supplied by many others. I am particularly grateful to the business people profiled in Part Three for their willingness to bare their souls so that others might profit from their experience. They are: Dom and JoAnn Parisi, Goose Cove Lodge; Anne Holliday, Anne Holliday & Associates; Addie Tarbell, TV Facts; Bob MacDonald and Bob Bergeron, Land & Sea; Warren Frank, New England Barricades; Rex Utsler, Grease Monkey; and Ursula Kruse-Vaucienne and Steve McCarthy, The Lobster Company.

For their technical guidance and timely suggestions: Fred Arnstein, Susan Galvin, Phil Bennett, Diane Levesque, Gary Ransom, Michael Chubrich, Robin Snowden, Alan Schnable, John Welch, and Kevin LaFond.

At AMACOM Books, I am indebted to Andrea Pedolsky, who recognized the need for this book and provided the opportunity to make it a reality.

Part One

Small-Business Ownership— What's In It for You?

1

The Natives Are Restless

Why American Workers Want Out of the Rat Race

American corporations in every industry are being rocked to their foundations by the winds of change—change so quick and so dramatic that many companies have been unable to cope. Companies that have dominated their industry for decades have found that what worked well in the past won't even keep them in the ballgame today. Giants like GM, American Express, IBM, United Technologies, Digital Equipment, Traveler's Insurance, Sears, Roebuck & Co., Raytheon, Harris Corporation, Texas Instruments, Borden, Greyhound, Chrysler, Lockheed, Rockwell International, American Airlines—these and many, many other household names have undergone traumatic changes.

What's scary is that there seems to be no end in sight. Rather than abating, the turbulence of the eighties is accelerating in the nineties. And the United States is not unique. Sweeping changes throughout the world are redefining the marketplace. The global economy has become a reality, erasing borders and obsolete economic controls. The prevailing emotion, from the boardroom to the mailroom, is raw fear. The most experienced executives in virtually every industry are struggling to find answers, often with little success. Many top managers have given up the goal of growing the business in exchange for strategies that they hope will allow the company simply to survive.

Nearly every major American company is committed to both cost cutting and downsizing, hoping to hold on and weather the storm.

Presidents and CEOs, when questioned in the privacy of their paneled offices, admit that they are scared and have few workable ideas about what to do to fix what's ailing corporate America. Listen to them in their own words.

> "The pharmaceutical industry is poised for a storm they are in no way ready to weather. The party is over. We'll no longer enjoy the 15 to 20 percent margins of the past. We have a national healthcare system out of control. It's got to stop. Unfortunately, drug companies are highly visible. We're going to be hit hard. Large numbers of highly paid managers will be axed. They don't even see it coming." *CEO, leading pharmaceutical company.*

> "I'm being paid millions to lead this company. People think because I occupy this office I must have answers. I'm scared senseless. I don't have any idea what will get us through this, and neither do my top people." *CEO, major U.S. airline.*

> "We are totally unprepared to cope with the dramatic changes in our industry. Even though we've improved impressively, it doesn't matter. Our global competitors keep raising the bar and increasing their lead. Our market share continues to drop. Our losses continue to mount. My guess is we will run out of time before we find an answer. Stockholders will take a bath, and many thousands will lose their jobs." *Executive vice president, auto industry.*

> "The entire industry is under siege. No one will survive without cutting large numbers of employees. The go-go days are over. We can't even predict how the industry will shake out. Nothing is sacred. Nothing is secure. I have no idea how to manage this company." *CEO, Fortune 500 financial services company.*

> "I was groomed to lead in a world that no longer exists. I was led to believe that cradle-to-grave security was our leading corporate value. I had always thought that no matter the problem, we'd find an answer. I lie awake nights thinking about the thousands of employees who will hear that their jobs will be eliminated because we have no answer." *Senior vice president, U.S. computer company.*

Large corporations evolved in an era of relative stability, when market variables were definable and predictable over time. Decision making and organizational design, planning, and control were created around assumptions that no longer apply. Today, this relative stability has been replaced by a state of chaotic stability. The implications for business are staggering. Corporations must not only redefine themselves; they must be able to redefine themselves continuously. And they must do so at low cost and with lightning speed. Not only is this not easy; it's expensive. Since most executives do not see that stockholders are willing to commit to the long-range investment required, the short-term focus is on surviving, rather than thriving.

If senior managers are unhappy, employees at all other levels are even more depressed and disillusioned. Millions who gave their lives to the company store have discovered that the commitment was one-way. Company loyalty, once a given in American business, has all but disappeared in many companies. American workers are realizing that their relationship with their employer is a financial relationship—period.

Employment security has all but disappeared. Although the corporate party line continues to be "People are our most important asset," the grim reality is quite different. Because America's top leadership has elected to pare costs by wholesale layoffs, mistrust and cynicism have skyrocketed at all levels, particularly among middle managers.

The problem is difficult. We do have far too many managers. Since empowerment and self-managed work teams have not been the norm for most large corporations, it has been necessary to hire hordes of managers to tell employees what to think, what to do, and how to do it. The corporate culture we've created has encouraged workers to hang their brains on a peg when they arrive at work and to pick them up on the way home. The message from management has consistently been, "I'll do the thinking, you do the executing."

In recent years many corporations have made a legitimate effort to push responsibility and authority down to the lowest levels. Therefore, far fewer middle managers are needed. Although in the economic downturns of the past employees at lower levels were the ones turned out on the street, today middle managers are the victims in increasingly large numbers. These formerly dedicated middle managers now realize that job security and career opportunity are a gamble at best.

The change in attitude has been truly astounding. Witness the following:

"I never realized the brutality of American business. I came in on Monday, and I was told to fire my entire staff by 3:00 P.M. But, I said, can't we space this out—give people a chance to find something else?

"No, I was told, we need to show the brass we're serious about cost cutting. It's them or us.

"I thought I was insulated from risk—that the company really appreciated my loyalty and contribution. Now I realize that 'people are our most important asset' was baloney. I'm viewed as having no more value than a forklift or a PC.

"I gave my soul to the company. I've paid a heavy price. I made a choice between my kids and the company. Not only was it the biggest mistake of my life, now I don't even have what I paid so dearly for."

Security aside, what about the quality of work life in corporate America? Most workers agree that it's getting worse. Working harder, longer, and with more stress has become commonplace. Although there are a few sparkling corporations that have created an exciting workplace for employees, the majority of today's corporate employees see a steady deterioration of their work life, with little hope for change in the foreseeable future.

It wasn't always this way. Except perhaps during the 1960s, Americans have generally viewed the corporate world as a desirable and secure domain in which to invest one's career. Hope for career and financial growth, if not always realized, was certainly believed to be practical and achievable. Today, that hope has been seriously eroded. In some fields (the computer industry, for example), hope has all but disappeared for many professionals. Performing a job without hope means a career without dreams. And without dreams, innovation, creativity, and the joy of work suffer terribly.

Hope is the foundation on which all human achievement rests. Our professional lives are no exception. The need to achieve, to grow, to see an opportunity for a better work life is what drives attitude, motivation, and ultimately, success. Otherwise, we create corporate zombies going through the motions and hoping only to hold onto their jobs. Pretty sad, isn't it?

You must ask yourself how much of this is true for you. Get your head outside your job, outside your company. Hover above it at 10,000 feet. Look down and observe your situation. What do you see? A vibrant meaningful job with opportunity for making a difference, a job offering career growth, a job offering the opportunity to realize your financial goals? Or is it something less than that?

For many, the stark realization that working in corporate America has become onerous, highly stressful, and often unstable is simply a reality they must learn to live with. For a significant number, however, resignation is not an acceptable option; nor is working in an environment that does not allow them to control their own destiny. They recognize that changing the situation from within is not practical. Opting out seems to be not only attractive but the only viable alternative.

What About Square Pegs?

For those of you who have known for a long time that you're not a corporate animal and never will be, there's little pain and turmoil in making the decision to go it on your own. But if you've spent most of your adult life playing the corporate game, it's not so easy. Are you a round peg in a corporate square? If so, that could explain why you've never been really committed and engaged in the corporate world.

Suppose you leave, only to find that it's the other way around—that you're a corporate purebred in an alien entrepreneurial world. Bad news, indeed. More than likely, however, you're a hybrid. Labels in any situation oversimplify; here, they're downright dangerous. Popular literature to the contrary, many people can and do survive and thrive in the small-business world even though they were very happy and successful in the corporate world. Very few of us are purely one thing or the other. Many of the interests, skills, and experiences acquired in the corporate world can be transferred to the small-business environment with relative ease.

The trick is finding the situation that fits you. Just as corporate cultures are radically different, the small-business world is full of colorful contrasts.

Where Does Opportunity Knock?

More and more, the opportunities are in the land of the small business. Big business requires a big market with an insatiable demand for more and more. Servicing the market requires an expensive infrastructure consisting of research and development, manufacturing, marketing, sales, distribution, customer service, and administration.

That's why big business places so much emphasis on market share. Without market share, the numbers don't make sense. In recent years, brutal international competition, recession, quality problems, and capital constraints have conspired to cause serious problems for big corporations. Big business built a cost structure based on faulty assumptions about the size and stability of the market. A hungry lion sucking up cash can cause big problems even for the largest companies. Unlike in a small company, which can change strategy and policy on a dime, in a large business it often takes years to work through the bureaucracy to enact the necessary changes.

Today's world has turned big business upside down. These lumbering giants are finding that their very size is a serious obstacle. Customers are demanding customized service, customized product, and lightning speed. Struggling to reinvent themselves, many of America's big corporations are in big trouble. And it's going to get tougher. All the experts agree. In an effort to get competitive, companies will continue cost cutting and downsizing for the foreseeable future. This translates into continued lack of security and decreased opportunity for those who work for big business.

What does this mean for small business? It means opportunity is shifting in favor of companies that can operate in the new world order. Small companies don't need huge markets to make huge profits. Niche marketing has the edge over mass marketing. Given the rising expectations for products and services that fit customers' wants and needs with precision, small business has an incredible advantage. Small size, formerly a liability, has suddenly become a competitive advantage.

In a volatile and quickly changing market, dominated by customers who expect a profound understanding of constantly changing needs, the company that can structure itself as an amoeba has an incredible advantage. Rigidity and slowness are just not going to cut it. The next decade will be an age of opportunity for small business.

2

The American Dream

The Benefits of Owning Your
Own Business

Almost everyone in the world of work has dreamed of owning his or her own business. The freedom, the opportunity for unlimited income, the chance to be your own boss, the job security, the status: All these and more are perceived as powerful incentives for running your own show. Like most things in life, there are two sides to the story.

There are many myths floating around concerning entrepreneurship and the world of small business. Most people are long on opinion and short on fact. Take brains, for example. The idea that highly successful business owners are somehow smarter than the rest of us is pure hogwash. Al McGuire, the brilliant sportscaster and former basketball coach, once said, "The world is run by C students." There is little correlation between academic achievement and success in running a business. Some of the most impressive business successes have been led by people who had little success in an academic environment. That doesn't mean they were stupid. Far from it. It's just that intelligence takes many forms.

And what about compensation? It's commonly believed that small-business owners earn less than their corporate counterparts. Well, yes and no. Although some do earn less, many do quite well, indeed. A recent survey by the marketing research firm Phoenix-Hecht discovered that of the 163 millionaires surveyed, 74 percent own their own businesses. According to the IRS, 89 percent of individuals who make over $50,000 per year own their own business. But that's not the half of it.

If you're simply an employee, you have few ways of sheltering your income from the gobble, gobble, gobble of taxes. Owning a small business is absolutely the best tax-avoidance vehicle around. Not tax evasion, tax avoidance. There's a big difference. Avoidance is legal; evasion is not.

While the name of the game in large, publicly owned companies is profit, the goal of most small businesses is to make little or no money. That doesn't mean the business owner isn't putting a lot of money in the bank. Quite the opposite. There are many ways of structuring personal financial gain as legitimate business costs.

For example, did you know that, as a business owner, you can pay each of your children up to $3,600 tax-free? What a great way to save for their education! Your compatriots in the wage world will have to pay with after-tax dollars. Business owners can also write off much of their entertainment, travel, insurance, subscriptions, transportation, phone, storage, even home expenses. And the list goes on and on.

Although what is reported as salary and profit in small, privately held companies may be modest, the actual financial benefit to the business owner may be substantial. Any small-business owner will tell you that it makes little sense to report high profits, which result in a huge tax bite that in most cases can be avoided. In fact, the average annual reported income of those millionaires I mentioned was only $137,500. How come?

There are many creative ways to funnel cash into the owner's pocket. That's why savvy accountants and business brokers look at small-business profit and loss statements with a jaundiced eye. The Mercedes, the condo at Killington, the trips to South America and Europe may all be legitimate costs of operating a business. There are literally hundreds of ways to live high on the hog while legally reporting a modest income.

That's why sophisticated buyers of small businesses pay little attention to profit and have a keen interest in a detailed analysis of the cash flow. It's not only what makes the business go; it's what enables business owners to live well.

What About the Risk of Failure?

Certainly there are risks. You've probably heard the story before. Although the statistics from government and private organizations that track business performance vary somewhat, it goes something like this: A third of new businesses fail in the first six months. Three-quarters within five years. Nine out of ten companies in existence

today will eventually cease to exist. It's possible to lose everything—
life savings, even the family home. Sounds pretty bleak, right?

But hold on. Things are not as bad as they seem. First of all, the
illusion of security with a large company is exactly that—an illusion.
Big corporations are hit as hard as small companies by recession—in
many cases, even harder. Just because you work for a large corporation doesn't guarantee eternal job security. And if you're a middle
manager, you have cause to worry more than most. The American
Management Association conducts annual downsizing surveys in its
7,000-plus members, the majority of which are large companies.
According to Eric Greenberg of the American Management Association, middle managers are being cut far out of proportion to their
members. Since 1989, although they make up 5–8 percent of the
employee population, middle managers have accounted for 19 percent of the layoffs.

Job security in the 1990s will become a dinosaur. Most workers
have come to realize that job security in a large company over which
they have no control is tenuous at best. The only real job security is
one's own competence practiced in an environment where one has
complete control. That makes owning and operating a small business
more and more attractive for the years ahead.

Alan Schnable, a writer and marketing consultant, observes:

> "It was a revelation for me to suddenly realize that I didn't
> have to get up every morning and go to work for someone
> else. The idea that you have to have a job is a concept that
> most people find difficult to rid themselves of. It just never
> occurred to me that I could go make myself a job or buy
> one. Once I accepted that creating personal cash flow was
> possible without the traditional concept of a job, a whole
> new world brimming with possibilities opened up."

But let's go beyond job security. Just how risky is small business?
The numbers are not all that they seem. Many business failures are
intentional. In fact, the owners of those businesses don't view the
dissolving of the business as a failure. Often the business was
conceived and developed as a temporary job replacement vehicle.
The owner had no intention of building an ongoing profitable company. However, when the company stops doing business, it shows
up in the statistics as a business failure. In other cases, the owner
tires of the business and decides to do something else. Another
business failure? You decide.

A disproportionate percentage of failures are retail businesses.

The odds of a new restaurant's surviving for even a year are very, very low. In all small-business retailing, ease of entry and cutthroat competition are facts of life. A variety of other factors, such as poor location, low margins, limited customer base, and undercapitalization, make retailing a risky venture under the best of circumstances. How many times have you driven down Main Street and asked yourself how long that new store would last?

The most significant factor impacting the high failure rate in retailing is by far the owners themselves. A high percentage are completely ignorant of even the fundamentals of business. And in an environment in which marketing expertise is the engine that drives success, it's astounding how many retailers have no marketing plan or even know that their business success depends on it. The landscape is littered with failed retail businesses. Unfortunately, there will always be a fresh crop of newly minted, starry-eyed retailers to take their place. Overconfident and underprepared, the majority will add their names to the long list of business failures.

Outside the world of retailing, the odds of success are markedly improved. Not that the business environment is necessarily superior. Rather, the business acumen of the owners tends to be more developed. Owners are more likely to understand how their industry works and what they must know to compete successfully. Sales, marketing, distribution, pricing, and product development are understood. A majority of business owners are experienced in the field before they venture out on their own.

These factors tend to stack the deck in favor of success. Unlike those in retailing, where the customer base tends to be fickle and can change loyalties overnight, most business-to-business buying relationships are more codependent and long-lasting. Business owners tend to be much more aware of the need to develop long-term partnerships with customers, and they develop their business strategy to that end. Since the cost of sale associated with creating new business in many industries is high, business owners place a heavy emphasis on customer retention. That means an emphasis on what matters to customers. The result is a stable of loyal customers pumping cash into the business.

All the experts agree on the most critical factor for business success. It's not the business. It's the people running the business. Even in industries in which the market is brutally competitive, some companies thrive. Southwest Airlines is a good example. While others in the industry struggle to hold on, Southwest makes money year after year.

And then there are those high (and some not so high) rollers who simply enjoy throwing the dice to see what happens. Believe it or not, there's a bunch of people out there who enjoy sowing the seeds of high-risk start-ups just for the fun of it. It's fun money, and, who knows, maybe the venture will turn out to be the next Microsoft. They know going in that the risk is unacceptably high, but, to them, it's like buying a lottery ticket. If it hits, they're rich. All those failures are recorded in the loss column.

According to Bruce Kirchhoff, professor of entrepreneurship at the New Jersey Institute of Technology, the survival rate for small businesses is much higher than is commonly believed. Over an eight-year period, he followed 812,000 firms with fewer than one hundred employees. While only 28 percent of the sample ostensibly made it, he found that for each of the eight years an additional 3 percent of those companies changed hands or changed the type of ownership either randomly or because of a decision by the owner. They hadn't failed at all. Therefore, what appeared to be an additional failure rate of 24 percent was in fact quite the opposite, and the actual survival rate was 52 percent, not 28 percent.

The lesson is this. Scary as the numbers seem, they don't mean what they appear to mean. When you eliminate retailing, high-risk dice rollers, owners who deliberately terminate their companies, and business incompetents, the risks of failing are reduced dramatically. The trick is to find a business that fits you and that has either a proven track record or great potential. Sure, it's not easy, but it's certainly possible.

If you approach the job of finding the right business for you with due diligence and intelligence, the odds are excellent that you will find a company that has a high likelihood of long-term success under your directorship and the potential for an excellent financial return, as well.

What About the Money?

Success magazine reports that the number of millionaires has been growing at three times the gross national product. Every thirty-nine minutes, a new millionaire is created. Where? General Motors, IBM, or Hewlett-Packard? Hardly. These new millionaires are the owners of small businesses. Through talent, hard work, and timing, they have parlayed their investment into a money machine. And right behind those millionaires are plenty of others who, although not worth millions, are doing extremely well.

If you've been a wage slave for a long time, you're certainly aware of the limitations and inequities of the system. Adherence to ridiculous salary or wage scales that who-knows-who created for who-knows-what illogical reasons are the norm. Although nearly everyone agrees that there's little relationship between what one is paid and what one contributes, few know what to do about it. In the interests of avoiding mutinies, wars, or worse, corporations impose a rigid compensation plan that seldom correlates with the worth of employees and that pleases almost no one.

With the exception of the very top management, most companies of any size severely limit employees' chances to get rich. The Hay Group, a Washington, D.C., compensation consulting firm, reports that only 3.3 percent of professional employees in large companies command more than $100,000 per year, and only a third of that group earn in excess of $150,000. No matter how hard one works, no matter how important or critical the personal contribution, the deck is stacked. And the reasons boil down to the compensation system. By design, it caps potential.

Even in commissioned sales, where there is more correlation between contribution and compensation, most companies place limits on how much an individual can make.

A dynamic salesperson explained her extended vacation in Jamaica this way: "Actually I'm through working for the year." When asked why, she said, "I sold my yearly quota twice over in the first four months. Since we have a cap on what we can make and I've made it, I'm taking the rest of the year off."

Stupid business policy? Yes. Unusual? Not at all. One hopes that some forward-looking company will snatch this dynamo up and pay her to produce all year.

If you've been frustrated by the limitations placed on your compensation, you'll find owning your own business refreshing. Gone are the ridiculous rules that shackle your potential. You have no limits and, of course, no excuses. Your compensation can be and will be in direct proportion to your contribution to the business's success.

But you will benefit not only from having no limits on your salary; you'll also open up whole new avenues of money making, often with even greater potential. Every dollar saved in taxes is equal to three dollars in revenue, and a substantial amount of that money can go directly into your pocket. That's why a savvy financial advisor must be a part of your management team.

Sooner or later, business owners realize that perhaps the greatest financial reward is not what the company is producing now but what it will produce later when it's cash-out time. It's like the difference between renting an apartment and owning a home. Even in today's market, home investment makes economic sense. Business ownership can make even more sense. Not only can you realize an excellent income from your business, you're also building equity. The more you grow the business, the more it's worth. Think about it. What will you have to show after a lifetime working for someone else? On second thought, maybe you don't want to think about it.

How much can you make annually from owning a small business? Here are some examples of the yearly owner's benefit, from just a few very small businesses. These are not in any way exceptional money-makers. In fact, they're typical, ordinary, everyday companies.

Engineering firm—12 employees:	$ 90,000
Christmas ornament manufacturer—2 employees:	$200,000
Marine aftermarket manufacturer—8 employees:	$ 95,000
Glass products manufacturer—3 employees:	$ 90,000
Automotive aftermarket manufacturer—5 employees:	$180,000
Aviation publication—1 employee:	$ 90,000
Greeting card publisher—2 employees:	$150,000
Management training company—22 employees:	$275,000
Construction products distributor—4 employees:	$130,000
Business consulting firm—4 employees:	$250,000
Industrial waste disposal company—1 employee:	$100,000
Communications equipment distributor—2 employees:	$ 75,000

Remember, these numbers reflect only the annual take. The increasing equity value of the business is added on top of that. It's not hard to see why, once the economics are understood, owning a small business is an attractive alternative to being a wage slave.

However, creating wealth, as opposed to making a living, requires a wildly different mind-set. It requires thinking about your career differently. It requires understanding leverage and how to use the talents and experience of others to make money for you. It's what owning a highly profitable small business is all about. And when the time comes for you to throttle back and enjoy the fruits of your labor, your business will pay back all you've invested and a great deal more. So if money is a motivator for you, owning your own business almost always provides the opportunity to make more of it.

What About the Other Rewards?

For many business owners, the money is secondary. The opportunity to make a difference in ways that matter to them is even more important. Creating good jobs, solving customer problems, developing an exceptional product, providing a training ground for people to develop skills and experience, and supporting the local business community are just a few of the important intangible benefits.

For others, the status of owning a business is very important. The chance to call themselves president, CEO, or head honcho is very gratifying. If that sounds funny and trite, think about how much emphasis is placed on rank and title in the corporate arena.

All around you there are highly successful business owners who have found the good life through their businesses. They have many reasons to prefer owning a company to working for someone else.

Ask yourself how many of the following statements hit close to home:

"I'm tired of taking orders."
"I'm tired of making a great deal of money for someone else."
"I'm tired of having my ideas ignored or hijacked by others."
"I'm tired of corporate political games."
"I'm tired of feeling no excitement on the job."
"I'm tired of making peanuts."
"I'm tired of meaningless work."
"I'm tired of not having an opportunity to make serious money."
"I'm tired of knowing my future is in someone else's hands."
"I'm tired of providing customers with second-rate products."
"I'm tired of wage caps, bosses, restrictive policies, and limited authority."
"I'm tired of settling for just a job."

Owning your own company is not without its hassles. There are many. However, they tend to be somewhat different from those just listed. Many highly successful business owners look back on their decision to strike out on their own as the result of an evolutionary process growing out of the realization that they were indeed sick and tired of the corporate merry-go-round. They usually vacillated for some time before realizing that things were probably not going to get better and that their feelings were not going to change.

But, having taken the plunge, most express few regrets. A Louis Harris poll of 2,000 business owners reveals that if given the chance, 78 percent of the respondents would choose to do exactly the same

thing again. Two-thirds of them consider themselves successful beyond even their own expectations. Interviews with hundreds of
business owners, even with some who are not particularly successful
financially, reveal that fewer than 1 percent would prefer to be back
in the corporate world.

What About the Job Itself?

If there's one word to describe running a business, it's variety.
President, janitor, finance director, lawyer, office manager, production supervisor, salesperson, personnel manager, marketing manager, quality control officer, advertising agent, bookkeeper, collections agent, customer service rep, director of research and
development, and shipping agent are all roles filled by most owners
of small companies. *Boring* and *repetitive* are not even in their vocabulary.

If you need to be in a highly structured environment where tasks
are clearly defined and predictably repetitive, perhaps you should
pass on running your own company. If, on the other hand, you have
a high tolerance for ambiguity, see undefined landscapes as an
exciting opportunity for creativity, and would rather lead than follow,
you'll probably find unprecedented fulfillment in running your own
show. Running a small business allows you to zero-base your career.
If you approach it intelligently, you can literally do anything you
want. Although it may take a while to reach your goal, you will
ultimately have the option of farming out what you don't do well and
what you find boring and distasteful, leaving you with the opportunity to do those things you find meaningful.

Over time, you'll realize that leading your company is much like
leading an orchestra. It's not necessary to know how to play the
oboe, violin, or french horn. Your job is to see that they are played
together to make beautiful music. If the opportunity to lead is truly
important to you, there's no better place to do so than in your own
company. Endless variety, the chance to make a difference for customers, the authority and the opportunity to lead—all come as part
of the package. No wonder most people never want to go back to the
limitations of the corporate world.

What About Family and Freedom?

Although many families have been torn apart by working together in
the family business, just as many have been deep-sixed by the

pressures and demands of the corporate world. Although it's certainly not for everyone, family businesses can be extremely satisfying. For many business couples, the opportunity to build something together provides an important sense of shared purpose. *In Love and In Business*, by Sharon Nelton (Wiley, 1986), is a wonderful book that describes the rewards and challenges facing spouses working together. If you have any intention of bringing your spouse into your business, be sure to place Nelton's book on your reading list.

For many, the most important reason for owning a business is the personal freedom it provides. To realize that one has the opportunity to create a life-style that reflects both personal values and interests is the ultimate high.

One business owner put it this way: "When I get up every morning, I'm unemployed. Nothing will happen unless I make it happen. And that's both scary and incredibly exciting. Realizing that I'm no longer subject to the whims of corporate fate, that I'm responsible and in control of my destiny, has allowed me to create a life for myself and my family that most people envy. My only regret about leaving the corporate world to own and run my own company is that I waited so long to do it."

3

How Now
Brown Cow?

Alternatives to Corporate Wage Slave

If the corporate world is no longer for you, what is? Buying and running an existing business is but one alternative. Assuming you are not independently wealthy and must bring cash into the coffers to live, you must somehow make a decision and go forth to earn a living. But what are the options? And what are the pluses and minuses of each? Let's take a look at the possibilities.

Hi-Ho Silver, Away!

Many of us enjoy playing the role of the Lone Ranger. Our idea of heaven is working alone—completely alone. Sarah is a good example. For twenty years she worked for a major oil company in the human resources department. Over the years she gained experience in every aspect of human resources management, from recruiting and selection to compensation, training, and executive development.

She left the corporate world in 1989 to work as a partner in a human resources consulting firm. Although the work was different, many of the old issues she had found so annoying in her old job were present in her new company, as well.

> "I simply changed partners. The change did nothing to eliminate what I hated about the job. Office politics, major decisions over which I had no control, the glass ceiling, and—worst of all—huge time chunks taken up in meaning-

less meetings and managing others were driving me up the wall. What I really wanted was the opportunity to make a difference for my Fortune 500 clients. Since I've spent my professional life working with large companies, I know exactly what the root problems are and what to do about them.

"I don't care about working with a team of colleagues. It just holds me back and wastes time. I work best alone. I know how to sell my services, and I have the required experience, so why not go it alone? So I did. And I love it."

For Sarah, the answer was to go it on her own. She just didn't fit as an employee in any company—large or small.

Another Lone Ranger who works as an independent manufacturer's agent shares Sarah's views. She reflects: "I just don't herd well. Trying to get me to conform to the rules and policies of any company is like trying to herd cats. It's impossible. You simply end up with a harried herder and an extremely unhappy cat."

In a sense, these people are running their own businesses. They call the shots, define the playing field, and decide how and where to expend their energies. But without them, there is no company. The only asset is themselves. Theirs are personal service businesses with little or no inventory or tangible product. If the owner gets sick, the business dies. What is often referred to as business goodwill is nonexistent. The business therefore has no equity value.

There's nothing at all wrong with that. For many, it's precisely the right career fit. And although there may not be equity value, the independent can still realize many of the tax advantages of any small business.

If the idea of being completely on your own, creating your own job, and living solely off your wits is appealing, this may be the option for you. But know what you're getting into. Many who thought this life-style was just what the doctor ordered found that in reality it was a lonely existence—so much so that they eventually found it necessary to come in from the cold.

Mark, a senior vice president of a regional phone company, observed:

"I was so sick of the bureaucracy of big companies. Home alone sounded like heaven. It turned out to be hell. I had never realized how much I needed the corporate structure.

> Without a boss, I just didn't have the discipline to do what
> was necessary. But the worst thing was the loneliness. It
> was like being in solitary confinement."

Perhaps the most critical factor to consider if you're going it alone is your ability to continually sell your talent. There's no one else to help out. And if you're not talented in the sales arena, you'll be in big trouble fast. In addition, this option has a limited upside. Although you may make an excellent living, you can't make big money because of your limitations as a human being. There are only so many hours in the day, and since it's impossible to clone yourself, once you've used up the available time either selling or delivering what you've sold, that's it; your income and your profit potential are maxed out.

What about a one-person firm with a product? You'll still be limited by your own finite stamina and time. The fact that you have a better mousetrap, although interesting, is often irrelevant. Business success depends on doing many things well, which doesn't apply to most of us. Even if you're insightful enough to discover a lucrative unmet need in the marketplace and create a nifty product to fill it, the manufacturing, marketing, selling, and distribution still have to be done, and done well.

Then, since most products have limited life spans, there's constant pressure to provide new products or product enhancements. Since there's no one else to take on some of these responsibilities, company growth peaks early, limiting the upside.

Creating a Start-Up?

Every year millions of new businesses are born. Beginning with an idea and a vision, entrepreneurs with a lot of hope and hustle create new companies, taking their shot at the American Dream. Starting with a clean slate means you don't have to deal with old company baggage or established ways of doing things. Restrictions caused by geography, obsolete product lines, and overpaid and underworked employees are all nonexistent problems.

You can organize the way you want, select the customers you want, or set up shop wherever it suits your fancy. In short, you can custom-design your company so that it meets personal as well as business requirements. There's certainly a lot of ego gratification in starting from nothing and building a profitable company that provides jobs and value to the community. If you really know what you're doing, this could be an exciting and rewarding way to go.

But consider the other side of the coin. The risk is higher. Start-ups consistently fail in far greater numbers than established businesses. And you have to do absolutely everything. It's rather like building an automobile as opposed to buying one. The question isn't can you do it; rather, it is should you do it?

Since you have no customer base on which to build, there's no instant cash flow to pay for business expenses or your salary. And since you probably have no product or service ready for immediate sale, you'll have to take the time to design and produce one. There are no experienced employees, no business systems or processes, no name recognition in the market. All this translates into a great deal of time with no money coming in and a good deal going out. You can almost always count on waiting a minimum of nine months to a year before there's much hope for a positive cash flow.

And then there's the energy required to start and sustain a new business, especially one that produces a healthy profit. Almost everyone drastically underestimates the enormous effort required. Sixty- to ninety-hour weeks are common, dragging on for months or years. If anything resembling a balanced life-style is important to you, think twice about a start-up. You must be willing to risk everything you have, all your money and all your time.

Purchasing a Franchise

John Naisbitt, business futurist and author of the blockbuster *Megatrends*, says, "Franchising is the most successful marketing concept ever created." It's true. The franchising concept has literally transformed companies such as McDonald's, Dunkin' Donuts, Midas, Jiffy Lube, Holiday Inn, AlphaGraphics Printshops, Century 21 Real Estate, Blockbuster Video, and Uniglobe Travel—all household words. Name recognition and reputation alone guarantee a critical mass of hungry customers from the moment the doors of a new franchise open for business.

With the exception of manufacturing, there are franchises for everything imaginable. Francorp, a franchise consulting firm based in Olympia Fields, Illinois, reports a total of 4,500 franchisors in the United States and Canada. Franchising employs over 8 million people in over sixty industries. Francorp estimates that a new franchise opens for business somewhere in the country every eight minutes. Studies by the U.S. Department of Commerce show that fewer than 5 percent of franchised businesses have failed in any year since 1974. That's impressive when compared to small-business failures in general. Franchise consultant Andrew Kostecka estimates that in 1992, not exactly a banner year for the U.S. economy, business-format franchises increased their sales by 6 percent to $246 billion.

In many ways, buying a franchise is like buying an existing small business with a proven track record. So let's examine this option in some detail. What you're actually buying is a proven system for generating sales and operating the business, with an acceptable (you hope) monetary return. Many franchisors provide a whole lot more. The best ones see you as a business partner and have a vested interest in your success.

In recent years many franchisors have made impressive improvements in the quality of service delivered to their franchisees. There are several reasons. Most have come to realize that a constant stream of lawsuits by franchisees is not in their best interest. Not only is litigation expensive, it turns away exactly the kind of buyers they wish to attract. Second, the caliber of individuals buying franchises has improved. The average buyer today is a forty-year-old college-educated professional with a net worth in excess of $300,000. An increasing number are corporate refugees with cash in hand and a strong commitment never to return to the corporate world. The franchise option is often attractive because it provides the opportunity to both own a business and take advantage of the wisdom and structure that an experienced franchisor can provide.

These affluent, savvy buyers are demanding that franchisors provide a level of support previously unheard of. The days of taking your money, giving you a week of training, and wishing you good luck is disappearing. The Federal Trade Commission has come down hard on many franchisors, and a number of states have tough new franchise regulations. Most industry watchers agree that the 1990s will see franchisors shifting their priorities toward long-term support and active involvement in the businesses of their franchisees.

Where Are They?

Perhaps one of the most overwhelming parts of investigating the franchise option is sorting through the mountains of information. Your first step is to get the view from 40,000 feet. Each year *Entrepreneur* magazine publishes a franchise guide describing and evaluating all major and many minor franchises in the United States. They also break out the top one hundred in terms of size: the thirty fastest-growing, the twenty lowest-investment franchises, and the thirty newest franchises.

The International Franchise Association runs franchise expos, essentially business trade shows, all over the country. It's not unusual for 50,000 people to show up for these events to get an overview of virtually all franchises that might interest them. You'll also find franchise ads in *The Wall Street Journal* and the business opportunities section of most major metropolitan newspapers.

Once you've selected a few opportunities that interest you, the real work begins. Investigating a franchise should command the same diligence you'd use in investigating any other business. In this arena, it's easy to get seduced. You'll be dealing with very good salespeople trying their best to entrance you with their offerings. You'll receive a well-oiled sales pitch, along with a slick offering prospectus.

This document, called the Uniform Franchise Offering Circular (UFOC), by law must contain twenty-three specific items of information regarding the business opportunity. But take care: Franchisors would have you believe it covers everything you need to know; it doesn't.

Because it is a great concept, franchising has boomed. However, along with the many straight shooters have come a sizable number of outlaws and incompetents hoping to ride the coattails of those who operate competently and ethically. The UFOC and state regulations have gone a long way toward exposing the bad seeds, but that's hardly enough. You must take the responsibility for analyzing the business opportunity thoroughly and for investigating a number of areas, both inside and outside the UFOC.

Beyond the UFOC: Evaluating the Offer

The offering circular and other sales materials address initial fee requirements, royalty payments, estimates of start-up costs, and working capital requirements. Many franchisees have found the estimated numbers considerably off the mark. That's why you need professional advisers working with you. Also, a heart-to-heart talk with a few current franchisees will be most enlightening.

The UFOC begins by introducing the franchise, its principals, and its litigation history. It also contains audited financials for the last three years. You and your accountant should study these carefully. They always tell an interesting story and often raise some questions that might never have surfaced otherwise. For instance, how much is being siphoned off as profit, rather than being reinvested in the business? How much does the franchisor spend supporting its franchisees? And, of great interest, how much is being spent in legal fees (a barometer of litigation frequency)?

Because franchise laws regarding claims about profit are very strict, it's difficult to obtain accurate data. In fact, by law, franchisors are not allowed to estimate how much you are likely to make. And since it's certainly one of the more significant questions you'll want answered, you'll have to dig that information out yourself. How? By visiting owners of several existing franchises.

Don't rely on the shortlist of owners recommended. Get the entire list, and make your own additional selections. Talking money is awkward, but after you've spent time developing rapport and trust, you must ask *the* question. You should come right out and say, "Pat, this may be uncomfortable for you, but I'll bet you had the same question when you were investigating buying in. What kind of money can I realistically expect to make? Of course anything you say to me is off the record and strictly confidential."

What else do you need to know? Here are some additional points to consider. Just exactly what is the product or service? Is it a fad? Believe it or not, there's a franchise for bungee jumping, and it requires serious money to get in. Now really, how long is that going to last?

Are you considering a swimming pool franchise near the Arctic Circle or a lawn-care franchise in New York City? Make sure your geography is appropriate for the kind of business you're considering. The reputable franchisors will help you make sure the market is there for your product or service.

Is the product manufactured by the franchisor or subbed out to a third party? If the latter, is this third party reliable? Does the franchisor assume warranty liability? How well has it responded to claims? Product liability is a serious issue today. If you should get sued, who pays? What are the competitive products in your geography? Are they superior or inferior? Does the product or service conform to your state's regulations and licensing requirements?

Management and Support

The most critical component of any franchise is the people behind it. Who are they? Examine the résumés of the people at the top and the people you'll be dealing with as you run your business. Is their experience what you'd like to see, considering the money you're putting on the line? What do they actually do? Are competent advisers actually out in the field supporting franchisees? If so, how? Will your new employees be trained by the franchisor? What is the specific content of the training and its duration? Is it on-site or at the home office? What's the commitment to ongoing training? Is there a fee?

What plans and strategy does management have for continually developing a competitive edge? How much is spent for developing new products and services?

This last point is extremely important in today's swiftly changing and volatile market. It is astounding how few franchisors spend serious time and money planning for the future. The ability to react swiftly to a shift in the marketplace is fine, but often too late. Companies that will thrive in the decade ahead, franchise companies included, are those that shape the market, not react to it. Unfortunately, many franchisors look at what worked in the past and then clone the old success model. All too often, the model created is soon a dinosaur.

Visit the corporate headquarters, and talk to the company's top executives. As they say, a picture is worth a thousand words. What do they look like—snake-oil salesmen or seasoned executives? What do they talk about? Are they frank and direct in answering your questions? Look at the digs, for sure. More important, look at the lower-level employees. Are they cream of the crop or bottom of the barrel? Ask the management the following three questions: "If you were me, what questions would you ask?," "What should I personally expect from you and your top executives?," and "Why should I buy this franchise?" By the way, if they're just too busy to see you, imagine what kind of help you'll get once you're in the field.

More on Fees and Costs

Most franchisors require an initial license fee. That's good for both parties. The franchisor should have a return on investment and the capital to set you up right and support you down the road, and the fee quickly eliminates buyer candidates who aren't serious.

Find out exactly what that fee includes. Can you pay in installments? With or without interest? Is it a one-time fee? Does the fee cover initial inventory, training, field support, and promotional assistance? What's the deal with royalties? Most royalties are periodic payments based on a percentage of sales. In many cases, the ongoing royalty payments cover such things as co-op advertising, centralized bookkeeping, and field training. Examine carefully all fees and costs. Are they required? Why are they necessary?

Many sadder but wiser franchisees have found that they were contractually obligated to buy inventory and supplies solely from the franchisor at inflated prices. Research every cost item that could appear on your profit and loss statement. Understand what it means to both your top and your bottom line.

Site Location and Business Territory

Where will you conduct business? Many franchises are operated from the home. Does your city or town allow that? If your franchise is retail, location may be the most critical factor in your success. The better franchisors are quite sophisticated at performing the market research required to ensure the necessary customer base.

Will you lease, buy, or build? Who negotiates the lease or the purchase, or who supervises the construction? You or the franchisor? Be very careful here. It requires experience to ensure that all regulations are met and that serious mistakes are not made. More than one franchisee has found the business turned out on the street when the landlord decided to jack up the lease cost or not to renew. Leases and subleases should parallel the franchise term and have acceptable renewal terms and conditions.

What are the boundaries of your business territory? Is it exclusive, or can the franchisor sell additional franchises in your backyard? Too many pigs at the trough can spell disaster for everyone. In the old days franchisors used to make sure that none of their other franchisees would sell in your territory. Antitrust laws being what they are, it's now unlikely that anyone will make that guarantee. Under what conditions can your territory be reduced? In some cases, if you're unable or unwilling to meet a specified quota, you forfeit your rights to the territory. If the franchisor plans to open a new franchisee close to your territory, do you have first rights to buy it?

Operating Policies and Requirements

Franchise agreements have lots of rules and requirements. You gotta do this; you gotta do that; you have to be open during these hours; you must run an ultraclean machine; you have to maintain this inventory level. Franchisors take their image and their identity very seriously, or at least the good ones do. Fail to adhere to Regulations A through Z, and you could find yourself in deep trouble. You may even lose your rights to the franchise. You must know the deal. Don't find out you can't or won't meet the requirements after you've mortgaged the farm.

Look at the equipment requirements. How often must it be replaced? If you have a storefront, what's required and what's flexible? Can you sell products other than those provided by the franchisor? Exactly what products and services must you purchase from the franchisor or designated suppliers?

If you decide to sell or assign the business, can you? It's not unusual for franchisors to impose limits here. Some franchisors have a buy-back policy or a right of first refusal. How is the worth of the business determined? Know the rules, and be sure you're okay with them. Almost all franchise contracts run for a specified time period. What are the renewal requirements? Suppose the franchisor decides it doesn't want you as a member of the family any more. Under what circumstances can it file for divorce?

Noncompete agreements are a usual part of franchise contracts. They restrict you from competitive activity during the life of the agreement and sometimes after. Many think that noncompete agreements are unenforceable. Not true. Although no company can unreasonably prohibit you from making a living in your chosen field, a well-constructed noncompete arrangement can prevent you from doing many of the things you thought you could.

If all this seems a little too much, think again. You're talking about one of the most important decisions you'll ever make, and about a lot of money. It's all part of what's due diligence for considering any business. Federal and state franchise disclosure law is specific, and violations will result in civil or criminal action. That doesn't mean you can simply relax and assume that what you read in the offering prospectus is gospel. Franchisors are not likely to tell you bald-faced lies. It's just that they often select their truths carefully.

Is It for You?

Buying a franchise frequently is the right decision. It has many advantages:

- You will have instant recognition, reputation, and customers.
- The franchisor will cover your inexperience and train you properly.
- The franchisor will help you implement a proven business plan.
- The franchisor will handle many of the complex legal, accounting, and tax issues.
- The franchisor will take care of developing new products and services.
- The franchisor can often reduce the risk of business failure.

- Whatever the problem, the franchisor has seen it before and has a solution.
- When it's time to sell, the franchisor may even help you find a buyer.

You will also give up a lot. If you're buying a business because you need freedom the way you need air, you may very well find a franchise stifling. Lone Rangers need not apply. The franchise route requires good soldiers. There are rules, there are quotas, there are reports to file; there are guidelines with which to comply. Many people find franchise life too restrictive. If riding the range on your own is your idea of nirvana, you may find you're just too headstrong for operating a Color Tile, Inc., Little Professor Book Center, or Peter Piper Pizza.

The franchise option is a logical route if your personality fits. The security of a proven methodology comes with the package. If you're lacking in business experience or the required talent to go it alone, it may very well be your best option.

Entering a Partnership

If you read the business section of your newspaper, undoubtedly you've seen numerous ads seeking business partners. Usually the hope is that you'll be able to bring capital and, sometimes, expertise. Or perhaps you've talked with friends or business colleagues about the possibility of striking out on a business venture together.

Someone once said that the one ship you should never get on is a partnership. Most insightful. Most partnerships don't work out. They are born out of emotion, with great expectations and little else. Over and over the scenario is the same. Katherine and Edith, friends for years, decide it would be great to be in business together. They get along great, and wouldn't it be just dandy? Probably not. It's partnershp for the worst possible reason.

Take Bill and Sandy, who had a solid ten-year marriage and separate successful careers. When Bill was laid off from his high-level management job, they both saw it as an opportunity, rather than a disaster. They bought a small distribution company supplying industrial gases. Sandy reflected, "We had talked and dreamed about running a business together for years. With incredible naiveté, we jumped in with both feet. Within a few months we were continually at each other's throat. Bill had always been the boss and assumed that would continue to be the case."

Bill agreed. "I treated Sandy like a low-level employee. Since I had industry experience, an overinflated ego, and a history of calling the shots, it never occurred to me that I would have to operate differently. We never sat down and decided who was responsible for what."

"It was Bill's condescending attitude and bullheadedness that got to me," commented Sandy. "Finally I'd had it. I had to admit I just couldn't work with him. We agreed that I'd leave the business and Bill would either find another partner or we'd sell the company. We sold to a competitor."

"It nearly wrecked our marriage," observed Bill. "I'd never consider another business partnership with Sandy. I love her too much."

To have a good chance for success, a business partnership should be thought through very carefully. First, you should ask why you're thinking about a partnership in the first place. Here are some common—but poor—reasons.

- You're friends and just love being together.
- You lack the self-confidence you need to make it on your own.
- You're lonely being in business by yourself.
- There's too much work for one person.

It's not that business partnerships can't work. Even if the principals are spouses, partnerships can thrive if the personalities meld and the roles and responsibilities are clearly delineated. The key is making sure the partnership is formed for the right reasons and has well-designed ground rules.

What are the right reasons? Many excellent partnerships are formed to take advantage of complementary skills and experience. The best situation is one in which the potential partners have already worked together for some time. If you're good at R&D and at managing a manufacturing operation, you don't need a partner just like you. A better choice would be a partner with sales and marketing talent or financial management experience who will round out the company. Look for a partner who will provide a natural division of labor and create synergy. Here's a laundry list of must-dos when considering the partnership option:

- *Discuss personal business objectives.* Sadly, many partners have discovered too far downstream that their personal reasons for being in business are vastly different. If Fred is in business because he wants to coast along and be able to write off his golf game and you're gung ho to build an empire, lots of luck. If you're interested in retaining earnings to grow and Fred wants the profit right now, there's going to be trouble. You need to talk and talk and talk until you and your potential partners have a clear understanding of what each wants out of the business.

• *Develop a three- to five-year business plan that describes precisely where you're going and how you're going to get there.* Among other things, the plan should highlight revenue and profit goals, as well as growth objectives. Will new partners be recruited? How many and when? What are the criteria for being considered? Will employees be considered for partnership? Under what conditions?

• *Agree on management philosophy.* Nothing demoralizes employees more than having to deal with partners who can't agree on how the workers are to be managed. Both authoritarian and participative management have their proponents. You must decide what's right for your company.

• *Define the division of labor.* Decide what needs to get done and who's responsible for getting it done. Over and over, partnerships fail because the partners didn't take the time to define and agree on key roles. Once roles have been defined, stay out of your partner's sandbox.

• *Develop a decision-making process.* Conflicts and differences will inevitably arise. How will disputes be resolved? Yelling loudest is not the answer. If there is an odd number of partners, decisions can be made by majority rule. If possible, however, strive for consensus. It may be that the partner who has responsibility for a given function has the final word in that arena. The point is, you have to agree on how to agree.

• *Define performance expectations.* Consultants who serve partnerships identify this as a common area of serious conflict. Partners who must carry others unwilling or unable to pull their own weight get very resentful. Partners who are workaholics often expect other partners to be just as driven. A frank discussion of policies governing work hours, time off, evaluating results against time spent, and personal business goals to be achieved by each partner all need to be covered. Are minimum standards expected of partners? If so, what are they? What happens if they are not met? How will partner performance be evaluated? By whom?

• *Detail the compensation plan.* Both salary and variable compensation are at issue here. When you own your own business, there are many ways to hand out financial rewards. You and your partners must agree on an objective set of criteria. How will stock be awarded? How will price be determined? Will partners be expected to loan money to the company? If so, how much and under what conditions? May partners borrow against their equity? If so, under what conditions? What are the terms?

Although you may not be even considering it when going in, an exit plan must also be defined. Cash-out provisions and buy-out formulas take on great importance when your equity is at stake. Under what conditions may partners lose their partnership status? What's the process for removing them?

Don't be intimidated by the long list of issues to be resolved. If these issues were routinely addressed before partners got married, the dismal divorce rate would improve dramatically. A partnership arrangement can be a wonderful way to own your own business. There's a lot to be said for sharing problems and responsibilities among partners who share the same dreams.

And often the odds of success are greater because highly skilled people are able to concentrate on doing what they do best. So if a partnership seems attractive, there are plenty of possibilities. You just need to be certain it's a good fit. The search techniques described in Chapter 8 are extremely effective at uncovering partnership opportunities.

Buying an Existing Business

Of all the options, the siren call of buying and operating a well-established and highly profitable small business holds the most appeal for many people—no partners to appease, no franchise inspectors or rules, and plenty of opportunity to build some serious equity.

From a financial perspective, buying a small business can make a lot of sense. Many small businesses are ridiculously undervalued. In addition to providing an excellent income, the cash flow from a well-run profitable business can often buy the entire company in just a couple of years. It's by far the best option for building personal wealth.

There's also the psychological aspect of owning an independent, established company. The idea of being a captain of industry, selecting the port, and steering the ship has great appeal to many. It fills a need that just isn't addressed by any other option.

Is it for you? Some people find it a nightmare. Many others for the first time in their careers hit their stride and find tremendous satisfaction and the financial reward they had dreamed of. To be successful, you must truly get a kick out of the business and have the necessary skill and experience to make it work.

A few years ago, thousands of people bought computer retail businesses because everyone knew that was where the future was, right? Many of these poor unfortunates knew nothing about the industry and, once in, found that they didn't like the business. When the market went south, they were left holding the bag without a clue what to do. Life savings went up in smoke. Those who had the experience to read the market and the skills to protect themselves survived. Many of them even sold their enterprises to naive dreamers who still believed the future was in computers.

The next three chapters are designed to help you avoid a similar plight. You'll learn how your past experiences and your current interests translate into the most appropriate business option for you.

4

Life Is Short

Do What Makes You Happy

Major life decisions are often guided by the realization that life can change or end dramatically and unexpectedly. Although everyone should certainly should think about building security and planning for tomorrow, it's also fair to live life as if it were going to end in a short time.

Perhaps living a life fully extended is easier when you have fully absorbed the reality of life's tenuousness. How each person responds to the realization that life is fleeting is rooted in a complex set of variables. For many, this reality keeps them centered on the priority of enjoying life. And since in our society a great deal of our time and a great deal of who we are is tied to our work, it naturally becomes a personal priority to enjoy our daily work thoroughly.

No matter how one makes a living, nearly everyone wants to feel that his or her job has meaning, both to the person doing the job and to society. Many people, however, spend every day wishing they could do something else. Every day is a meaningless grind rewarded only by a weekly paycheck.

Such people spend their lives not living but anticipating living. They believe that someday, somehow, in some way their lives will be transformed into fulfilling, happy existence pervaded by true meaning and satisfaction.

Of course, it never happens. The interesting thing is that many of these people have limitless options. They are highly educated, with skills to match, and could have it all. Probably you have friends and acquaintances who fit this profile. Monday through Friday, they plod through dull, joyless jobs, living for weekends and vacations.

When you think about it, it's utterly insane. What a tragedy; what a misuse of a life. And yet, millions elect to stay in situations they find distasteful and meaningless and that offer no hope of improvement.

So why this philosophical discussion on the meaning of life? What difference does it make? It makes all the difference in the world! If you're reading this book, you're one of those who've said, "Is that all there is?" and answered with a resounding "No!" Further, you've decided, at the very least, to investigate an option that you find fresh and intriguing—owning your own business.

Well, think long and hard about this. If chucking the rat race has become a priority and you think owning your own business is your ticket to job fulfillment, doesn't it make sense to be sure that business of yours delivers exactly that? It should get you popping out of bed, excited about taking on the challenges of your business day. It should bring pleasure, fulfillment, and meaning to your work life. And you should be able to say truthfully, "I'm really happy."

Examine your motives. Are you simply trying to escape a bad situation in the blind hope that owning a business might be better? Stop right here. Don't press on in with this idea until you're satisfied that you're truly committed to this quest for the right reason.

It's okay to escape a situation that no longer meets your needs. Just be certain that, in addition to *escaping from*, you're *moving toward*. Finding, buying, and managing a business is a big job. Not unpleasant, just big. It also has a huge financial impact on you and your family. When you consider it, doesn't it make a whole lot of sense to make sure that this new business of yours is really your ticket to job satisfaction, as well as to financial success?

It may well be that owning and operating your own business is exactly right for you. But how do you really know? Is it just a feeling in your gut, or do you have reasons that you can articulate? Do you even know what to look for? And if you do, do you know how to evaluate objectively whether you've found it?

All the stuff you've heard about some people being "corporate types" or "entrepreneurial types" does have a good deal of truth to it. It's also true that dumping people into one or the other of these two buckets is overly simplistic. Many people who don't fit the entrepreneurial profile have happily succeeded in their own business.

Determining What You Can Afford

Before you get too far downstream in your quest to move into the world of business ownership, you should step back and take stock of who you are and where you are in your life. This chapter gives you some tools to do just that.

Don't give this part short shrift. It's the foundation on which a successful search for the right business for you rests. What good is it to own and manage your own business if it results in unhappiness or worse? What good is it to set your heart on a business that doesn't fit your skills, interests, or pocketbook? It's great to reach for the stars, to go after a business that sets your heart aflutter. However, it's also important to keep your feet firmly planted on the ground. The business must match up with the skills and experience you can bring to it, as well as with the price you can afford to pay for it.

First and foremost, you must get specific about what you can realistically invest. That number drives your decision concerning the top dollar you can afford to pay for any company.

The majority of small businesses do not sell for cash. If they did, very few would ever get sold. In fact, it's common to finance about two-thirds of the sales price. That leaves you with a down payment of the remaining one-third. Obviously, there are many exceptions, but use this as a rough guideline in your search for a high-profit business. A rule-of-thumb called the Rule of Two-Thirds states: "The cash flow must service a debt of two-thirds of the sales price." In other words, after paying all the expenses associated with running the company, enough money must be left over to meet the payments due on the debt incurred to buy the company.

If you're coming up short, it's not a high-profit business. You may still decide to buy it, but bear in mind that you'll have to increase the down payment or increase the number of years the note runs in order to reduce the annual debt service. Otherwise, the numbers won't work. Remember, one of the most attractive benefits of buying an existing high-profit business is that it provides you with an income and pays for itself as well.

Complete the financial statement on page 37. It serves several purposes. First, once you know how much cash you have available to invest in a business, multiply it by three, and you will have a rough dollar estimate of the size business you can afford.

Second, you'll need to provide this financial statement to a seller when you start getting serious about a deal. Most sellers will want assurances that you're a financially qualified buyer. So get your personal financial statement prepared now.

And, by the way, sellers often run a credit check on a buyer before they agree to act as the bank in financing a note to buy the business. Check your own credit rating. If there's a problem, and mistakes are not that unusual, you need to deal with it now.

Confidential Financial Statement

NAME _____ **DATE** _____

ADDRESS _____

INCOME

Salary   _____

Spouse's Salary   _____

Dividends/Interest   _____

Other Investment Income   _____

Other Income   _____

TOTAL INCOME   _____

LIABILITIES

Real Estate Mortgages/Notes   _____

Other Long-Term Debt   _____

Short-Term Debt   _____

Other Liabilities   _____

TOTAL LIABILITIES   _____

ASSETS

Cash   _____

Securities, Stocks, Bonds   _____

Real Estate   _____

Household Furnishings   _____

Automobile(s)   _____

(continues)

IRA, Retirement, Profit-Sharing	_____
Cash Surrender Value Life Insurance	_____
Loans/Notes Receivable	_____
Value of Business Owned	_____
Other Assets	_____
	_____
	_____
TOTAL ASSETS	_____
NET WORTH	_____
Total Liquid Assets Available	_____

The three major credit reporting firms in the United States are Credit Data in Orange, New Jersey; Credit Bureau, Inc., a division of Equifax, in Atlanta; and Trans Union Credit Information Company in Chicago. Although you'll find others listed in the Yellow Pages, most of them are subscribers to one of these three firms. Ask your banker how to get your credit report. Better still, ask the banker to run the check for you.

Assessing Your Business Profile

You also should assess your personal business profile before you take the plunge and buy a business of your own. Although very different types of people thrive in the world of small-business ownership, they seem to have certain characteristics in common. If you're not like them, you certainly should know now before you burn your bridges. Keep in mind that there's nothing wrong with you if you find out that business ownership is not for you. The fact is, it's not for most people. We're all unique and require different environments to be happy, successful, and content. That's what makes the world go around.

Although no test can predict with complete certainty how well-suited you are for running your own business, you can gain some insight into your probable success by comparing your business personality characteristics with the known characteristics of successful business entrepreneurs who have happily and successfully owned and managed their businesses for years.

The Small Business Personality Profile that follows will help you get a feel for just how suited you are for your anticipated venture. If this exercise is to provide you with meaningful information, don't kid yourself. Be brutally honest. Answer the questions by describing how you really are, rather than how you wish you were or how you think you should be. Ask several people who know you well (your spouse, for example) to verify your judgment by answering the questions with you in mind. No matter how honest you are, it's doubtful you'll be able to be totally objective about yourself. If your judgment is the same as that of several people who know you well, great. If it's not, you'd be wise to get further information by having five to eight people rate you using this exercise. Try to select people who not only know you well but know you well in a business environment. You might think this is overkill. But you're talking about how you're going to spend your life.

Small-Business Personality Profile

On a scale of one to five (with five being the highest), evaluate yourself on the following:

_____ 1. I'm a self-starter. No one needs to get me going. I see what needs doing and do it.

_____ 2. I work harder than most people I know. I'm willing to work long hours even if it means sacrificing in my personal life.

_____ 3. I have a desire to win. I'm willing to do more than most to make certain that I do.

_____ 4. I have a high tolerance for uncertainty. I can work effectively even when the outcome is not clear and the work process is unstructured.

_____ 5. I have a nose for numbers. I understand how they impact a business.

_____ 6. Most people consider me a leader, rather than a follower.

_____ 7. My experience tells me I have good judgment when it comes to finding the right answer, even when the problem seems insoluble.

_____ 8. For as long as I can remember, I've been goal-directed.

(continues)

_____ 9. My friends would agree that I'm persistent. Once I've set my mind to something, I don't quit until it's done.

_____ 10. I'm profit-oriented. I love to make money.

_____ 11. I see risk as an opportunity. Since I've been a child, I've been willing to stick my neck out.

_____ 12. I'm comfortable with the concept of survival of the fittest. I can think of many times when I've deliberately placed myself in situations where the outcome depended solely on me.

_____ 13. I can fire someone when I need to without procrastinating.

_____ 14. I've got good marketing instincts. I often see opportunities that others don't. And usually I'm right.

_____ 15. I can deal with conflict effectively. If a decision needs to be made, I confront it even when I know it won't be pleasant.

_____ 16. I seldom get sick. I hardly ever miss work because of illness.

_____ 17. I have something to prove to myself.

_____ 18. I have a high level of self-confidence. Everyone else thinks so, too.

_____ 19. I'm an independent type. Some people may even call me stubborn.

_____ 20. Opportunity is much more important to me than security.

_____ 21. I'm a good salesperson. I can usually convince people to see things my way.

_____ 22. My spouse supports me and my business goals 100 percent.

_____ 23. When I experience defeat, it makes me even more determined to win the next time.

_____ 24. I'm willing to risk a lot of money even if there's a possibility I might lose it all.

_____ 25. I have a lot of self-discipline.

_____ 26. I can handle stress. Most people say that I perform well under stress.

_____ 27. I've always been willing to go without for now in exchange for reward later.

_____ 28. I'm street-smart. I understand business and what it takes to make a buck.

_____ 29. I'm willing to do whatever needs to be done in order to have my own business, including working harder than others.

_____ 30. I work well with people. My coworkers consider me a good person to work with.

If your score was 100 or above, your profile is much like other successful entrepreneurs'. You will probably be very happy owning your own business.

If your score was between 85 and 99, you have a good chance of success, provided you work hard to cover the areas where you're weak.

If you scored below 85, you would probably find running your own business an unfulfilling experience. Even if you were successful, it just would not be "you."

Keep in mind that we're talking about your personality profile here—whether you have the psychological makeup to succeed and enjoy small-business ownership. We're not talking about required skills or experience. Chapter 5 has more to say about that.

Identifying Your Wants and Don't-Wants

The final exercises in this chapter will assist you in nailing down exactly what your interests tell you about what businesses will turn you on or off. You need to identify what you want and what you don't want in a job. First, identify those things that you know you should avoid, the things that could bring you misery and leave you disillusioned. What are they?

Think about this carefully. Go back over your work history, and identify the unpleasant parts. Also look at those situations in which you did not do well. Was it the result of lack of knowledge, lack of interest, or both? To get you started, how do you feel about commuting? Have you ever left a job because the commute was getting to you? How about travel? Do you love being a road warrior or hate it?

What kind of relationship do you want to have with employees? If you're buying a fast-food company, you'll have to deal with constant turnover. You'll find yourself having to fill in for employees who didn't show up for work. Is that okay with you? Maybe you need employees who are on the same level as you, professionals whom you see as colleagues.

How do you feel about long hours, including nights and weekends? If you're looking at a retail business, sixty hours or more a week, including weekends, is not unusual.

If your work history indicates that you don't do well in direct sales, that tells you something about types of businesses you should avoid. How do you feel about managing others? Is it a joy or a pain?

Do you like dealing directly with customers, or do you prefer to work behind the scene?

How important is business status to you? Do you get great satisfaction out of an impressive office, support staff at your beck and call, a fancy title with a well-respected company? Or do you find the whole thing a drag?

And what about time? In a word, it's your life. How much of it do you want to spend in your work?

Identifying what you don't want helps drive your decision concerning what business is right for you. On your "No" list, record what you want to avoid in your new business.

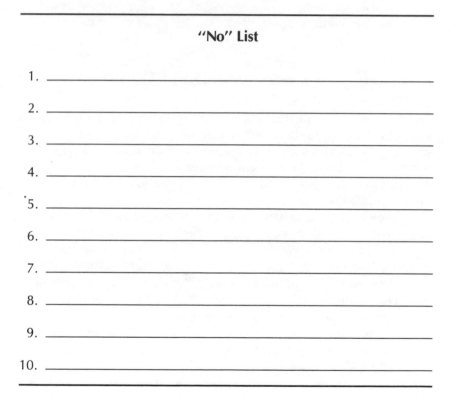

"No" List

1. _____

2. _____

3. _____

4. _____

5. _____

6. _____

7. _____

8. _____

9. _____

10. _____

Determining the Ideal Job for You

If you're to be truly fulfilled by business ownership, the daily grind must be supplanted by joy in your job. The Ideal Job exercise will help you identify the actual components of daily work that most closely suit your interests. This is important because different kinds of companies require very different talents from their owners. A retail operation that caters to upscale professionals is very different from a small manufacturing company serving the giants in the computer industry. A fast-food franchise is radically different from a small publishing company or a country inn.

Remember to focus only on interests in this exercise. Assume that you're eminently qualified in every field. The issue of your skills is addressed in Chapter 5.

Step One: Create Your Perfect Job

Sit down at your word processor or with a clean notebook. Assume that you can wave a magic wand and create the perfect job for you. Don't get sidetracked by reality. Reality has nothing to do with this exercise. This exercise works only if you reveal your true desires, unbiased by practical considerations. Treat it like a fantasy.

Think about that ideal job in terms of thoughts and activities, rather than responsibilities. What would you actually be doing? As you begin to visualize those activities, begin to "free-write" in detail what you see. Record both what you're doing and your thoughts. Free-writing is nothing more than rapidly recording your thoughts and the pictures that form in your mind as they occur. Don't be concerned with grammar, quality of writing, or even whether it makes sense. Just write as quickly as you can, and let it go where it wants to.

Beginning with the first activity of the day, follow yourself around for the entire day, capturing every activity and the thoughts accompanying them. Whatever you do, don't make judgments such as, "This is silly, totally impossible, highly self-indulgent, and completely unrealistic." None of that matters. When you finish, you'll have several pages. Don't read what you've written. Simply put your work aside for several days.

If you have trouble getting started, if you are just drawing a blank—just start writing. Write whatever thoughts you have. It might look something like this:

> I feel foolish as hell doing this. These books are all so unrealistic. They dream up stuff like this to fill pages. I suppose it won't do any harm if I fill a few pages. Can't hurt, might help. I wonder what having these thoughts says about me? Well, for one thing, I probably wouldn't be

happy writing, publishing, or selling this kind of baloney. But now that I think about it, I do like the idea of creating something: a product, something solid. Something that will last. Something I can point to with pride and know that I'm responsible for its creation. I remember as a little girl, I was always making something. Mom always said I'd end up bringing beautiful things into the world. Gosh, I remember those quilts I used to make. What a joy it was to dream up the design and see it come alive in an actual product. And I guess I enjoyed making the quilt as much as designing it. Everyone always said, whether it was quilts, clothes, or even those coffee tables, it was the best they'd ever seen. I just loved it! I wonder how I got so far afield? God, I hate accounting! Maybe I should think about a small company that manufactures a product I love, like furniture. Not a bad idea. And I know a lot about it. Now let's see, just suppose I did own a small furniture manufacturing company. Here I am on my way to work Monday morning. It's April, and the tulips are in full bloom in front of the plant. I love beautiful things. I guess I'll check on how the design is going on the new recliners. Probably spend an hour or so with Frank and Judy ironing out the technical problems with the design. They will be so gorgeous if we can only figure out how to reinforce that frame! Nobody thought we could solve the problems with the bunk bed design. Now everyone is copying it. I'll have to scramble if I'm going to make my plane to New York. I love showing off the new line. I could spend all my time just talking to the buyers. I get so excited when they get excited. But then there are so many things about this business that I love. Maybe I ought to write those down. But I must get back to the day. What would it look like if a video camera were recording my activity? Well, after that design meeting, I'll get Tom to drive me to the airport. That will give us a chance to talk about the winter marketing plan. I'll be darned, maybe this exercise does have some value. Where was I? Oh yes, the winter marketing campaign. I'll need to check with Tom about . . .

Now that's not so hard, is it? There's no such thing as writer's block. The trick is to just get your hand moving and keep it moving. Start writing anything, and before you know it, you'll be producing exactly what you need here.

Step Two: Create a Second—and Third—Perfect Job

After a week, perform exactly the same exercise with one important change. This time, when you wave that magic wand, you can create any ideal job, *except* the one you created last week. When you've completed the second writing exercise, wait a week and repeat the exercise to create a third ideal job.

Step Three: Look for Patterns of Likes and Dislikes

After a few days, carefully read all three free-writing exercises. Something quite remarkable will happen. Although the jobs may be radically different, you'll see a definite pattern of the same kind of activities over and over. Embedded within those activities are the key job components that excite you and make you happy. Pull them out, and write them down. Then write a job description that closely describes your role and responsibilities, using your ideal job components. You may find it useful to go back and reread the example, circling key words and phrases.

If this exercise is not working for you, you're allowing your inhibitions to block out the real you. Tell them to take a hike, and try it again. As you begin to think about the business that's going to excite and sustain you, it had better have a healthy number of the components you've recorded. After all, one of the reasons you're leaving the rat race behind is to find job fulfillment, isn't it?

When the time comes to evaluate your fit for a specific business opportunity, the work you do here will be valuable. It will ensure that you don't lose sight of what it's all about—finding a business that will be exciting because it dovetails with your interests. Since you now know exactly what to avoid and to seek out in order to be happy, it's a simple matter to analyze any situation you're considering and ask yourself, "Is there a match?" If not, maybe you can make some changes to bring things more in line with what you know you need. If this is not possible, do you really want to proceed?

The lesson here should be obvious. Buying a business that ends up forcing you to do the things you hate doing and prevents you from doing the things you love is utterly insane. Yet thousands of people just like you will continue to buy businesses that bury them in misery and despair. Fortunately you don't need to count yourself among them.

Being engaged in a business of your own that truly reflects what excites you is wonderful. But it's not enough. The business will also require a set of abilities and skills from its owner. Making sure there's a match is the objective of Chapter 5.

5

The Right Stuff

Matching Experience and Skills With the Right Business

Now that you've given some serious thought to your interests and how they relate to business, it's time to give equal consideration to what your experience tells you about the talents you can bring to a business.

Most small businesses flop because the business owners didn't have the required skills to make them fly. Strange as it may sound, most people who put their entire life savings on the line to buy a business give little thought to whether they have the skills to manage and grow the business. Listen to Janet Blanding.

"I bought my business two years ago. I had hit the glass ceiling and decided enough was enough. Since I'd always been attracted to the idea of owning a service business, the insurance business seemed ideal. I'd be working with a professional clientele, helping them make intelligent decisions concerning employee benefits and smart investments. The previous owner was a CPA before she bought the agency. She took it from less than a million to over five million in less than six years.

"It seemed like a gold mine. She was making an impressive amount of money. I felt that if she could do it, I could do it. After all, I was bright and had a proven track record in business. As a vice president of research and development, I'd taken many new products from concept to market, a task that certainly required complex skills. What I found, however, was that those skills had little to do with running a successful insurance agency.

"To my horror I discovered that I had absolutely no head for numbers, which was the key skill required in the business. No matter how hard I tried, I just couldn't seem to get it. As I think about it now, the fact that I had difficulty even balancing a checkbook should have waved a red flag.

"My customers were senior executives who expected a skill level I just didn't have. I quickly lost credibility and then their business. The agency, under my management, is failing. I don't know what to do. I've lost my savings. I hate my job. I've developed high blood pressure. If I had only known what I was getting into."

The sad truth is Janet could have known. Unfortunately, she did not understand the need to identify the critical skills that drive success in a business. Nor did she understand how to assess her skills and compare them to what was required. Unlike large businesses, where there is often a wealth of complementary talents, small businesses rise or fall mainly on the talent of the owner. Therefore, it's important to identify the specific skills that will make you or break you as a business owner.

Another sad example is Andy Wendall, an accountant by training. Andy spent twenty-five years working in financial management for three companies. He ended his corporate career as a vice president of finance for a well-known hotel chain. He reflected:

"Like many boomers, I came to the realization that the opportunity for further advancement was slim and getting slimmer. I decided to take my winnings and seek greener pastures. I bought a franchise that markets financial advice to small companies. Everyone I talked with said I'd be a natural for this business. I checked out the franchise thoroughly. It was financially sound, and the franchise owners I investigated were very successful.

"I was so stupid. My investigation focused on everything except what drove the business—sales. I couldn't sell my way out of a paper bag. To be successful, I'd have to spend at least 40 percent of my time hustling business. I just can't do it. I'm a numbers person, not a people person. This

mistake is going to cost me more than $100,000, not to
mention putting me out of a job."

Before you even think about the possibility of putting your hard-
earned dollars on the line, you must have a detailed understanding
of what knowledge and skills make the business tick. What does the
owner need to know? What must the owner be able to do? What
needs doing that employees can do? Identifying who needs to know
how to do what, when, and how well is not merely interesting. It's
essential.

It's astounding how many people get involved in businesses for
which they are totally unsuited. Just because the business matches
your interests perfectly doesn't mean it's a good fit for you. Although
it's not necessary to be highly skilled in every discipline that a
particular business requires, you must be sure that the areas where
you are weak are covered by employees or outside advisors who do
possess the required skills.

Who Are You?

If you're typical, it's been a while since you reflected about what you
have to offer. On the other hand, it's probably not all that unfamiliar
a concept. Any successful job hunt usually means that you were able
to identify and match your business skills and knowledge with the
requirements of an available job. Even though your experience may
not match the job perfectly, the required skills and knowledge base
may transfer very well. Your goal now is to match your transferable
skills with the requirements of your business. That means you have
to perform two assessments: an inventory of your skills and knowledge and an analysis of what the business requires. First, let's look
at you.

The Personal Business Profile

A simple tool to use for a self-assessment is the Personal Business
Profile. On the worksheet that follows, simply place a plus sign
beside your strengths on the list. If you are very strong, use two
pluses. Place a minus sign where you're weak. Again, use two minus
signs for the areas in which you haven't got a prayer. Then write a
one- or two-page personal business profile in narrative form, describing your strengths and weaknesses.

Personal Business Profile Skills and Knowledge Checklist

General Management Skills

_____ supervision
_____ hiring/firing
_____ delegation
_____ managing change
_____ incentive management
_____ personnel
_____ inventory control
_____ data processing
_____ manufacturing
management
_____ purchasing
_____ collections
_____ quality improvement
_____ debt financing
_____ written and verbal
communications
_____ customer service
_____ product development
_____ research and
development
_____ training

Financial Skills

_____ forecasting
_____ bookkeeping
_____ cash flow
management
_____ planning/budgeting
_____ tax law
_____ accounting

*Sales and Marketing
Skills*

_____ market analysis
_____ territory planning
_____ marketing research

(continues)

_____ sales management
_____ niche marketing
_____ negotiating
_____ distribution
_____ closing
_____ pricing
_____ sales plan
      development
_____ advertising (creative)
_____ advertising (strategy)
_____ merchandising
_____ sales presentations
      (one-on-one)
_____ sales presentations
      (group)
_____ prospecting
_____ telemarketing
_____ consultative selling

Now the important part. Each and every time you're reviewing a prospective company, take this narrative profile out and see if what the company needs is what you have. (You'll learn how to know what the company needs later in this chapter.) If there are glaring disparities, do not proceed with serious negotiations until you've worked out a plan to ensure that the company is safe from your inexperience.

The Business Background Summary

There's one more step to take in your assessment. If you were searching for a good job, you'd construct a résumé. In much the same way, a Business Background Summary helps both the business buyer and the business seller see that there is indeed a good fit between you and the business. Here's an outline of three simple steps to help you develop your own Business Background Summary.

Step One: Record Your Accomplishments

Write a chronological history of your work experience. Divide each job into sections according to the work performed, and write out what you accomplished in each job section. What counts is not what you did but what happened as a result of what you did.

For instance, suppose your job was marketing manager. What you did was to design and install a new marketing plan. The result was a tripling of sales within twelve months. Remember this acronym: **JAR**. It represents the Job you performed, the Action you took, and the Results you achieved. Use this acronym to help you evaluate your own achievements.

Step Two: Analyze Your Skills

Study each section of your job analysis, and extract the skills and areas of knowledge developed. Prepare a list of your skills and knowledge. This is your personal talent bank. It's what you can offer to the company you will own. Compare it with your skill/knowledge assessment as indicated in the Personal Business Profile. The skills should be pretty much the same.

Step Three: Write Your Summary

Prepare your Business Background Summary along the lines of Figure 1. Obviously, the details will be different, but the goal is the same—to highlight your skills and to document your achievements. Now that you know exactly what you have to offer, it will be much easier to see if your background is a good match for the company you're considering.

The Company Skill Assessment

Now that you've drawn a bead on what you have to offer a business you'd consider buying, you must know how to do a complete analysis of the prospective company to determine the knowledge and skills required to run that business successfully.

Fortunately, it's not as mysterious a procedure as you might think. A process called High-Performance Modeling, used by leading management consulting firms, can give you exactly what you need. It's an interview-and-analysis process that allows you to build a business performance model of employee knowledge and skills.

If you don't have a model that identifies what people actually do annually, monthly, weekly, and daily to guarantee business success, you're flying blind. You have no blueprint for success. And because your success will ultimately depend on what you as the business owner actually do, you'd better have great insight into the specific skills required to do the right stuff.

Figure 1.   Business background summary.

Emma Michaels
123 State Street
Brackett, WA 98041

SKILLS

Sales	Sales Management
Marketing	Marketing Management
Finance	Project Management
Quality Control	Operations Management

BUSINESS EXPERIENCE

1981–1992
Chief Operating Officer   Amalgamated Inc.   Cleveland, Ohio
Acted as president and chief line officer. Developed a cost reduction plan that decreased operating expenses by 32 percent, returning the company to profitability after eight straight years of losses.

1972–1981
Vice President, Marketing   Turnkey Systems, Inc.   Atlanta, Georgia
Responsible for all marketing in U.S. and Europe. Designed marketing plans for the company's eight divisions. Revenue growth averaged 30 percent in six of the eight. Developed a marketing research system to drive new product development, resulting in twenty-seven new products in three years.

1968–1972
Sales Manager   Rubbertech, Inc.   Atlanta, Georgia
Managed Northeast U.S. sales force of twenty-six and four regional managers. Developed the company's first formal sales training program, installed a sales forecasting system, and hired and trained all sales managers. Increased sales from 2MM to 20MM in four years.

1965–1968
Sales Representative   General Plastics, Inc.   Atlanta, Georgia
Sold injection molding systems in the South and Southwest. Sales were 400 percent over projections for 1968. Number one in sales for three of four years.

EDUCATION   Cornell University   Bachelor of Science   1965

Understanding the High-Performance Model

The trick here is to have a profound understanding of what the current owner of the business you're considering actually does that makes the company consistently successful. You'll find that simply asking that question outright seldom gets you the answer you need. Most owners simply haven't given it much thought: "Hey, if it's working, why do I need to analyze it?"

Your job is to help the owner analyze his or her own competencies in terms of what actions occur and what skills are required to perform those actions. You do this by using a special interviewing technique designed to get at what that business owner actually does to succeed. You'll be surprised to find that it's often quite different from what he or she thought.

Developing the Model

The interviewing technique described in this section may sound simple, but it isn't. Unlike other interviews you may have conducted, you are not asking what the interviewee thinks about such and such. You do not want opinion or perception. You want to know what actually happened. Here's how to do it.

Explain that you want to view the business as if you were actually watching the owner's actions over time. It's as if you were recording those actions on video. Begin by asking the owner to take you through a recent month describing what daily actions took place in sequence.

Are you getting the picture? That's exactly what you should be seeing. A living moving picture, depicting the events and actions of daily business over a month's time. If the activities and actions are dramatically different month to month, you'll need a broader angle to capture a complete cycle. As the owner talks, take notes—lots of them. Later you'll be able to use them as a prompt to replay your mental video. All of this will take several hours, but it is well worth the time invested. Since the business seller will probably be holding a good deal of paper on the business, there is, or should be, a great motivation on his or her part to ensure your success.

You're not finished yet. Next, ask the owner to identify three or four typical business successes over the last couple of years. What you're doing here is focusing in on actual case studies of success. You might think it would be difficult to remember the specific details surrounding these cases. It almost never is. Once the pump is primed, the only trouble you'll have is getting the owner to shut up!

A word of caution. How you do this is critical. It's easy to get suckered into gathering a good deal of opinion about what drove success, rather than recording what actually happened. The actual words you use will control the quality of what you get. Here's how it should go.

> "Holly, I really appreciate your taking the time to do this. Since I know little about the insurance business or what it takes to run an agency, this will be invaluable to help me intelligently approach the issue of buying your business. I'd like to start by understanding the big picture—what you do day to day that translates into your impressive results. I'm looking not so much for your opinions at this point—not that I don't value them—but what I need right now is a clear picture in my head of what actually goes on over, say, a month. What do you actually do when you show up for work Monday morning? I'd like to capture exactly what you're doing hour by hour. Does that make sense?

It should make a lot of sense if you've framed it correctly. The output of this inquiry should be pages of detailed notes painting an accurate picture of what this highly successful business owner actually does hour by hour, day by day, month by month. The next step is to develop the specific case studies we just mentioned in order to document the specific actions that lead to specific successes.

> "Deedy, I'd like to narrow this down a little more. I want to get an understanding of exactly what you did to get results in a specific case. That will help me to see precisely what you've done to make this business go. I'd like you to go back over the last couple of years and identify three or four situations where you felt particularly successful— situations that not only typify the routine in the business but also illustrate why you've performed so well."

For each situation, you should collect detailed information capturing the actions, thoughts, and results. Again, your questions should sound like this:

> "As you remember this situation, please give me a detailed chronicle of exactly what happened—what you said, what the customer said, what you did, what you thought about,

how you decided what to do next, and so forth. I'm just going to listen and take some notes. Could we start at the beginning? Set the scene for me. When did this happen? What was the context? Who was involved? What was the first thing to happen? What were you thinking at the time?"

You'll find that once the owner gets going, the detail will flow. Don't offer any opinions. Just keep the story going. Your questions should be confined to things like: "And then what happened? If I were recording this with a video camera, what would I have seen and heard next? What were you thinking at the time? What did she say? What was your response? What did the customer do? Tell me more about that." The key is to stay away from questions that ask for interpretation or perception. As Sergeant Jack Friday would have said, "Just the facts, ma'am."

You may be thinking that this will take a lot of work. You're right. But how valuable it is! You now have the raw material to construct a model of success for the business. And it's a model based not on someone's opinion or guess but on actual facts. You've even got case studies to back it up.

Don't stop now. As soon as possible, analyze what you have. For each of the three or four cases, you should have captured the critical incidents or events of the case, the reported thoughts and the reported behaviors. The next step is a thematic analysis of each case. What are the major themes that point to the key tasks of the job? What did that owner actually do, and how did she do it to achieve that outstanding result? What general and technical knowledge did that owner have that was critical to success in that situation?

If you've read Peters and Waterman's *In Search of Excellence*, you'll find this concept familiar. Essentially, these authors say that if you can find out what the best people are doing and then do the same thing, your probability of success is greatly enhanced. Makes sense, doesn't it?

Building the High-Performance Model

You're now ready to do the really exciting part—identifying the secret to getting results in this business. Start by rereading your notes for the first case and mentally running through the interview. Write down what seem to be the critical events that drove results in this case. Then list the specific actions and key job tasks for each event.

Your job here is to identify the critical few. You'll probably have a lot of events, but some are more important than others. For each critical job task, write down what actual knowledge and skills were used.

Go through this process for each case. Develop a summary for each case as follows:

- What were the critical events?
- What were the critical actions?
- What were the critical job tasks?
- What critical knowledge was required?
- What were the critical skills?
- What underlying thinking was critical?

You're almost home now. Reconstruct the first interview, the one you did to get a bird's-eye view of the business. Answer the same questions, and create a summary. Then place them all side by side. Assuming that the cases actually reflect typical critical situations, the summary data should support the summary of your first interview. They're just more specific.

One more step, and you're done. Compile one master list defining the critical job tasks of the business owner, followed by a sublist capturing all the critical knowledge (both general and technical), the critical skills, and the critical underlying thinking required to perform those tasks. You now have a performance business model that defines the specific actions and skills that drive performance for the specific company you're considering. And the case studies document it, providing you with even more valuable data. Not only can you say with confidence, "I know exactly what I must do to get the results I want in this company," you also have documentation indicating how much time should be spent on each task.

You know what to do, how much time to spend doing it, and what knowledge and skills are required. Talk about valuable stuff! Management consultants charge millions of dollars to big companies to do what has just been described. Companies pay for it because it works. And it will work for you.

Now that you have an inventory of your skills and abilities and an in-depth understanding of the skills and abilities that led to success for the owner of the company you're considering, it's relatively easy to see how closely the two match up. With the data you developed in Chapter 4, you now have everything you need to select a company that will bring great job satisfaction and long-term economic reward.

You have a good handle on how your interests accord with the kinds of businesses that will excite you. You have a detailed inventory of the skills you can bring to your company. And you have a highly effective analysis process that will nail the secret of success for your company.

6

Tying It All Together

How to Factor in Geography, Life-Style, and Money

If you've completed the exercises presented so far, you're probably anxious to cut to the chase and to search out the business that's just right for you. But before you charge ahead, there are still important issues to consider.

An important factor for many people is location. Although, for some, place of residence is unimportant—Boise or Boston are all the same to them—for many others, where they live is critical. Sometimes it may be more important than how much money they make, the job title, or even whether they buy a business. If you have roots in your community, do you really want to pull up stakes and move on? On the other hand, maybe you're ready to move on; maybe you feel that a change in scenery is just what the doctor ordered.

There are really two questions to consider—first, what's right for you, and, second what's right for the business. Let's talk about the second question first.

Geography and Business Considerations

Location may or may not be critical to a business. If you're considering a company that serves a customer base all over the country and perhaps overseas as well, you have lots of options. It's not necessary to be near your customers. However, you may find that cost of labor, rent, heat, and taxes will dictate where the business should be located.

In most retail businesses, location is critical—so critical, in fact, that it will make you or break you. Many people have made the mistake of locating a retail establishment where they wanted it, rather than where it should be. Although most people are aware that relocating a bathing suit boutique from Key West to Anchorage is probably a risky move, an astonishing number of business owners continue to locate their retail businesses in exactly the wrong place.

Sometimes even a few yards can make the difference. Listen to Paul:

> "I had always wanted to run a convenience store. I found a beauty located on the major artery leading into and out of the city. It was highly profitable, and revenues were growing steadily. I scooped it up. Since it was on the west side of the expressway heading out of the city, the rent was high. When the lease was up, I relocated about a quarter mile away on the east side of the expressway. The rent was a third less.

> "It was a disaster. My business plummeted. I'm barely able to stay alive. Finally, I called in a consultant. She took one look and said, 'Your problem is location. You're on the wrong side of the expressway. People don't buy their milk, bread, and beer on their way into the city. They buy them on the way home. There's no way they're going to buck traffic to make two U-turns just to do business with you. Relocate.' "

Although location in retail is critical, many nonretail businesses are relatively easy to relocate. Service businesses that serve a wide area are often quite mobile, assuming critical employees are also willing to move. Moving a manufacturing company with a large amount of heavy equipment may be prohibitively expensive.

When considering a move for the good of the business, keep the following in mind:

• What major cost reductions would I realize? Consider things like utility rates, cost and availability of labor, cost of the lease or purchase of real estate, taxes, shipping, and proximity to vendors. Many communities are willing to offer very attractive tax incentives, even to small companies, if they bring jobs to town.

• How is the business climate? Some states are more probusiness than others. Some communities have friendly business regulations; many don't. Be especially aware of zoning, EPA requirements, and the complexity of getting through the permitting process if you have plans to expand.

• Are the human resources available? If your business requires professionals or skilled blue-collar craftspeople, is the area capable of producing them? Are the employees you'll need likely to find the region attractive? Is the cost of living stable and compatible with your labor force? If your potential employees can't afford to live in the area, it may be difficult to staff your operation.

• What does the future of the area look like? Is it on the way up or down? What is the local political climate? Is it likely to support your business interests long-term? For example, a business related to aviation that depends on the local airport may be out of business if the local noise-pollution lobby has enough muscle to close down the airport.

The point is that the decision about where your company is located should be grounded in data about what's good for the business. However, since people do not live by bread alone, personal considerations are of equal importance. No matter how critical it may be to the health of the business, do you really want to live where you're unhappy? If you just can't live without the ballet, the opera, and gourmet restaurants, would you be happy in a small town a million miles from the city?

Geography: The Personal Side

There are people who would live on the back side of the moon just to have the opportunity to run a business. For many others, however, no matter how attractive the business may be, there's just no way they'd consider relocating. Take a look at yourself. Is this an important consideration for you? People who have moved around a lot know how they feel. If you've lived most of your life in one place, it may be difficult to decide about moving; you just have no frame of reference.

Jackie and Bob had spent their entire lives in a small town on the New Hampshire seacoast. When they closed a deal to buy a small winery in California, they felt they had achieved a lifetime goal.

Jackie recalled the move to the West. "We were so excited. It was like pioneer days, striking out for the land of opportunity. The kids were grown and on their own. We had a clean slate, a chance to build a brand new life-style. It was great for the first few months, but after a while we had to admit we were desperately unhappy."

Bill agreed. "It wasn't the business. It was going great. We slowly began to realize that we had chucked everything that was important to us. We both loved New Hampshire, especially the coast. It was home. We were fish out of water in California."

If you have young children, the decision may be more complex. You may be perfectly willing to live in some backwater, but do you want to send your kids to school there? And is it an environment where you want your kids to grow up? How does your spouse feel about it? Is he or she willing to give up a job, family and friends, a home, and a familiar and loved life-style to support your great adventure?

This is not the kind of decision you make off the cuff or without enthusiastic support from your spouse or life partner, that is, if you value the relationship. To you, your business may be the top priority. It probably is not your family's. They deserve to be involved in any decision that may dramatically change their lives. If the tables were reversed, wouldn't you insist on being involved in a decision of this magnitude?

Diane Levesque, a therapist whose practice focuses on family issues, frequently sees the fallout associated with new business ventures: "Many people fail to understand the personal consequences of the life-style changes associated with going into business or buying a business. By the time I see the victims, they're exhibiting symptoms of severe depression. Usually it takes a crisis of some kind for them to realize there's a problem. Often it's a spouse who pulls the plug on the relationship.

"When you run your own business," Levesque observes, "the environment encourages those with workaholic tendencies. Most don't realize what they're doing to themselves or to others."

Levesque offers the following to would-be business buyers: "Instead of talk, talk, talk, listen, listen, listen. Most people will say they discussed the decision thoroughly with the family. That's almost never true. The problem is compounded by spouses or significant others who want to offer their support, so they don't raise their concerns.

"And don't hear what you want to hear. Hear what's actually being said. Then go beyond what's said to what's meant—the issue which needs resolution."

Living the Good Life

Assuming that one of the primary reasons you're buying a business is to improve the quality of your life, it's a good idea to give serious reflection to defining exactly what that means. When you think about it, it's probably the single most important issue to address when taking the leap into business ownership.

If you're this far along in investigating the possibilities open to you, you must feel that there's something missing in your current work situation. Otherwise, you wouldn't be reading this book in the first place. Since the world of work and personal life-style are so inextricably tied together, you must look not only at how you'll spend your time at work but also at the inevitable changes that will occur in your personal life-style, as well.

For instance, most successful business owners spend much more than forty hours a week at work. If you're an avid golfer who values all that time spent at the club, are you comfortable giving it up to run your business?

The issue of time is tremendously important. All of us as we grow older realize how quickly life goes. How do you want to spend the time that you have left in your life? The job of running a small business requires stamina, long hours, and a willingness to give up things. As you think about the balance you want and need between work and personal life, what things are you willing to give up?

Levesque observes, "I see it over and over and over in my practice. People consistently fail to assess the personal implications of managing a small business. For many, the price was very high." You can be sure it will change your life-style. The question you need to address is, how?

Listen to Stewart and Debra, married and owners of a personnel consulting firm. "We lived and breathed the business," remembered Debra. "It took over our lives. We had no time for family or friends. Nights and weekends were never sacred. The nature of the business demanded being on call constantly. What was scary was that we couldn't let up if the business was to succeed. It was eating us alive."

Stewart agreed completely. "It was affecting our personal relationship. Even away from work, all we talked about was the business. I had no time for flying our small plane, which I loved dearly. Debra had no time to read or spend in her garden. The children were not getting the time they should have. Looking back, we should have seen the price we would have to pay, but we were so focused on growing the business that we never once asked, 'What is this going to do to us?' "

Or take Larry, the owner of a charter service with three boats and six employees. "I hated my old job as a sales manager. I spent my life on the road and lived for the weekend to get out on my boat. I thought long and hard before I finally decided to buy the business.

It would mean a radical change in the way we lived. When I finally bought the charter business I thought I'd died and gone to heaven. It's like playing full-time and getting paid handsomely for it. My life is completely changed.

"Marge and the kids love it too, especially living in Florida. Some of our customers have become very close friends. Sure, as in any business, there are the usual hassles, but I'd never go back to the way I used to live. The whole family has benefited, and every day I have to pinch myself to believe this is really all true."

Owning and managing a business can affect your life-style in a hundred ways, both positive and negative. Although you may not be able to predict every change in your work and personal life, you should be able to identify the most significant factors.

The following worksheet, a Life-style Profile, will help you to evaluate the wisdom of buying a business.

Unless you're single, make this a family affair. Let everyone affected by the decision have his or her say about each question as appropriate. After completing the discussion, summarize the conclusions on paper. Most important, use those conclusions to aid your decision making.

Sad to say, many people reading this book will not invest the time and energy required to complete this exercise. You're urged not to be one of them. Sure, it may be difficult to sit down, lay all the cards on the table, and be totally honest. But think about the risk if you don't. If you go through with the purchase of a business, you're not the only one making a sacrifice. Your whole family is making a sacrifice. And they're making it for you, with no assurance of any personal gain. The very least you owe them is to hear their concerns and to allow them to have input.

What if you don't? Well, if things don't work out, a business down the tubes may seem small compared to what else you may lose.

The Question of Balance

Some wise person once remarked, "When you're on your deathbed, you'll never say, 'I wish I'd spent more time down at the office.' " So why do people work themselves to the point where their lives become wildly out of balance?

Perhaps some of us have learned our lessons all too well. Certainly, ambition and hard work bring psychic, as well as monetary, rewards. However, when life becomes work to the exclusion of leisure

Life-Style Profile

1. What are the top three business reasons to buy this business? What are the top three personal reasons for buying the business?

   _____

   _____

2. How will running this business affect your relationship with your spouse or partner? What will you have to do differently?

   _____

   _____

3. If children are involved, what are their issues? How will they be affected?

   _____

   _____

4. If the business should fail, what are the consequences? Are they acceptable?

   _____

   _____

5. What leisure activities will be affected? How?

   _____

   _____

6. What improvements in life-style do you want? Will owning this business help you realize them? How?

   _____

   _____

7. Will belt tightening be necessary? Where? For how long?

   _____

   _____

8. Where do you want to be in five years? How will you get there? What's the price for each family member?

   _____

   _____

9. Is your life partner going to be involved in the business? As a subordinate or as an equal partner? Define the job responsibilities of all involved parties.

   _____

   _____

10. How will you balance your personal life and your business life?

_____

_____

_____

activities and relationships, the inevitable result is sadness and regret later on.

Marion is typical. "I was so proud of my business. We grew at better than 50 percent for five years in a row. One morning I woke up and realized that I had no relationship with my husband, and my kids were growing up without me. For the sake of the business, I had sold my family.

"I started delegating a good deal of decisions to my employees and cut way back on the time I was devoting to the business. To my surprise, the business has not suffered. The jury is still out on whether or not I can reclaim my family."

Balance, or the lack of it, largely boils down to how you spend your time. As you evaluate any business, one of your primary concerns should be an accurate assessment of the time required to run the business. Will it allow you to lead the life you want? Be aware that the answer is sometimes no. Sometimes it's possible to make changes that lead to greater balance, but, if it's not, you may, like Marion, wake up one morning and find you've paid a heavy price.

One of the exciting things about owning your own company is that you're calling the shots. You have complete freedom to organize your business life any way you want. Here are some questions to consider as you analyze the time requirements:

- How much time per week do you want to devote to the business?
- How much time is the current owner devoting? What's the industry average?
- What is being done that adds no value to the business? How much time does it require?
- Are there key employees who could take on additional responsibilities?
- Are there activities that can be subbed out to save time?
- Is it possible to save time if efficiency is improved? How?
- Is it possible to combine leisure activities with business activities?
- What would happen if you worked one day less per week?

What About Stress?

A little stress seems to contribute to both motivation and accomplishment. However, more and more evidence is accumulating that excessive stress is very bad news. The medical community recognizes stress as a significant factor in a large array of both psychological and physiological illnesses, including depression, heart disease, and cancer. Since the mind-body relationship is so crucial to health, it's wise to assess the degree to which the business you are contemplating is likely to contribute to your stress index.

How much stress is owning this business likely to produce? That depends on you. Stress is perceptual. What is extremely stressful for one person may produce no stress at all in another. In fact, what you find overwhelming, your counterpart in the company you're evaluating for purchase may find downright bracing!

It's not just a good idea to identify the situations under which you experience high stress. It's critical. Your happiness and health depend on it. Look back at your work and personal life, and think about the specific situations when you experienced a high degree of stress. Perhaps you freak out when you're confronted with an overwhelming number of tasks with limited time to complete them. Or perhaps you find working in an unstructured environment that requires rapid-fire decisions with little margin for error more than you can take.

You may be able to make the required adjustments in the business to ensure that you avoid your heavy-duty stress triggers. But first you need to know what they are. So write them down.

Here's a list of situations that many small-business owners have found to cause high levels of stress:

- Not enough money to cover the monthly operating expenses
- Business growing too fast
- Problem employees
- Problem customers
- Problems with vendors
- Questionable business practices
- Lawsuits or threat of lawsuits
- Problems with accounts receivable
- Perceived or real incompetence
- Being spread too thin
- Brutally competitive environment
- Insurance problems
- Business life and personal life out of balance

- Uncertainty or risk of failure
- Lack of family support

To what degree are these or other personal factors that you find stressful a part of the company you're considering?

Money: How Much Is Enough?

Without question, owning a business is a great way to make money. But how much do you really need to be successful, secure, and happy? It's oh, so easy to buy into the myth that wealth and fulfillment are related, even though we see evidence to the contrary all around us. A recent study of big-ticket lottery winners in the state of Maine concluded that, out of seven winners, not one reported being any happier as a result of having hit the jackpot.

The great thing about money is that it allows you the freedom to do those things that you find enjoyable and meaningful. If accumulating a fortune is meaningful to you, fine. If there are other things that are important in your life, don't let your business suck you dry for the sake of toys or for more money in your investment portfolio.

Fred owns and operates a company that distributes fire control systems. "I had a vacation home at the beach and one in the mountains and no time to use either. My kids were in private schools a thousand miles away. I never saw them. I drove a Mercedes and spent my life on airplanes and in hotel rooms.

"Two years ago I decided this was no way to live. I downsized the company, closing all five field offices. I'm making less than half of what I used to make, and I'm happier than I've ever been. We live comfortably, and I work a normal five-day week. The quality of my life has improved beyond belief. I'll never again get caught in the money trap."

The key here is good financial planning. Maybe it will surprise you to know that most Americans have no financial plan or budget. They have never seriously thought about what income level is acceptable. Usually there is a vague feeling that what they are currently making is not enough and that more would be better. They spend money randomly on things that bring neither joy nor return on investment. Even those who have more than enough to satisfy the needs that are important to them often continue to want more.

Often, those who have a compelling urge to buy a business, when pressed for their motivation, have no more reason than, "I'm not making enough money" or "I want to get rich." Crazy, isn't it?

If you take the time to sit down and determine what kind of money you need for the future and for the present, life will be so much easier and more secure. And, of course, you'll be in a much better position to decide whether a prospective business is right for you from the financial perspective.

Once again, if you have a spouse, make sure he or she is your partner in the planning. If you need the help of a financial planner, there are many good ones. Select one who charges a fee, rather than one who is free but whose purpose is to sell a bevy of financial products.

Happiness Is a Decision

Many people find that addressing the issues presented in this chapter is difficult—more difficult than any other aspect of transitioning to the world of business ownership. The return on investment, however, is out of all proportion to the time and effort required. The payoff is finding a business situation that gives you the satisfaction you want.

What if you don't do this? Then you are leaving your personal happiness to pure chance. It's no exaggeration to say that buying and running a business is deciding what to do with your life. You can decide, or you can let chance decide. Who knows, maybe you'll get lucky.

Now that you know how to evaluate which businesses match up with your interests and skills and dovetail with your personal requirements, let's move on to the task of actually finding that business.

Part Two

Your Business: Finding It, Pricing It, Buying It

7

Operating in the Dark

Why Most People Fail to Find the Right Business

Talk with any brave soul who has preceded you down the trail of locating and buying a profitable business and you'll find the process was not what was expected. If you're just starting out, you should know that it will probably take a lot longer than you think to find the business for you.

You'll also find that the road is full of obstacles and that attaining your goal is by no means guaranteed. It's been estimated that fewer than 25 percent of those seriously searching for a high-profit small business ever reach their goal. For those who are successful, it often requires years to locate and buy a company.

But before you chuck the whole idea and resign yourself to eternal damnation as VP of paper shuffling at good old Amalgamated, you should also know that your dream of locating and buying your own high-profit company is not a pipe dream. Every year, thousands of people achieve that very dream.

Locating a company that fits your skills and interests, fits your pocketbook, and returns the required profit isn't easy at all. Companies like this are not likely to be hanging on a tree in your front yard. But they are out there—if you know where and how to look. This chapter provides you with proven techniques and tools not only to find the business that's right for you but to do it with the least possible amount of frustration and wasted time.

First, it's necessary to define the playing field, identify the players, and understand the rules of the game. We start with the premise that the business of buying and selling businesses is one of utter chaos and confusion. The key mistake that many would-be buyers make is to assume that there must be a logical system that brings together motivated buyers and sellers on a level playing field, where everyone understands the rules of deal making. One need only adhere to the rules and proceed logically through each step to arrive at a win-win deal where buyer and seller shake hands, sign on the dotted line, and sally forth to enjoy the fruits of their efforts.

The fact is that nothing could be further from the truth. Let's take a look at the way it really is. And then let's compare that to the search methods that the majority of buyers employ.

The Hidden Business Market: The Difficulties of Finding It

First, let's assess the market. The reason you're having such difficulty finding a profitable business is that you're looking where it isn't! Your business is located in what is termed the hidden business market. This is the market where businesses are never publicly advertised, a market that is seemingly impenetrable except for the few professional buyers who know the ropes.

The vast majority of high-profit small businesses that are for sale are never advertised. Long before they go public, savvy buyers with an inside track snatch them up. Let's look closely at why traditional search methods are so ineffective.

The typical business buyer is not a professional buyer. Instead, he or she is likely to be a first-time buyer like you—a first-time buyer without an experienced practitioner to light the way, a buyer who is essentially on his or her own. And typically, the strategy is quite predictable. The result is a long and frustrating experience.

The first step that most people take is to cruise through the newspapers. Your metropolitan Sunday edition will have a fairly extensive Business Opportunities classified section. It usually begins with an extensive number of display ads extolling the virtues of a variety of franchises in fast foods, auto service, quick print shops, and the like.

Moving down the page, you'll note that the rest of the listings seem to be restaurants, dry cleaners and laundromats, video outlets, gas stations, convenience stores, and other small retail establishments. You turn the page, thinking, "Okay, let's get to the good stuff. Stuff like small manufacturing companies with interesting products, product distributors, professional service firms, or whole-sale suppliers." To your dismay, there don't seem to be any. Perhaps you skipped a page? You double-check. Nope. They're just not listed!

Sorry to say, you're right. They certainly are not listed. But how can that be? You know they're out there. You know people who work for them. You've even done business with them. And certainly those business owners get tired, get sick, have a falling out with a partner, and grow old and retire, and therefore have an interest in selling out.

Of course, you're right. They are out there. They do have an interest in selling. And they do sell. Only it doesn't happen through public channels.

Why the Best Companies Are Never Publicly for Sale

Let's consider why the most desirable companies are the hardest to find. First, very successful companies that you'd like to buy all thrive in large part because of their image and reputation. They have built excellent relationships with customers and suppliers. And they have excellent employees who are responsible for a good deal of their success.

Suppose customers were to get wind of the fact that the company was on the block. More than likely, they'd get very nervous and begin to ask questions like: "Suppose the new management doesn't take care of us like old Tom does?" "Suppose they raise prices?" "What if they move the plant and can't meet our delivery schedule?" "What if they sell out to a big company and they decide we're small potatoes?"

It's not at all unusual for old customers to decide suddenly that it's time to sign on with a second supplier "just in case," or to jump ship completely. New customers are not likely to feel comfortable signing on when they have no idea how they'll be treated by the new management.

The company's suppliers suddenly get edgy, and some even decide it's time to raise prices and rethink terms. Employees are frequently traumatized, so much so that morale and productivity are almost certain to suffer. And the competitiors just love it! "What, you're doing business with them? You should know they're bailing out. Selling the whole shebang. Who knows where they'll be in three months!"

So it's obvious that the last thing a seller wants to do is to go public. She knows the damage to her company can be serious. Without a doubt, she knows several horror stories that illustrate all too clearly the consequences of the sale's becoming common knowledge.

The owners of the businesses you saw advertised in the Business Opportunities section of your newspaper are not generally as concerned about confidentiality. Employees are usually less involved in management and have high turnover. Customers tend not to care who owns the business, and vendor issues are minor. These sellers are looking for buyers with basic business qualifications, not highly educated and skilled professional managers. A newspaper is a good medium for reaching the masses.

You probably noticed that some of the ads in the Business Opportunities section were run by real estate brokers. Remember that real estate brokers are in the business of moving real estate, not selling businesses. If your interest is in real estate speculation, great. If not, you probably won't find your company here. Sellers of profitable, desirable companies are highly unlikely to use a real estate agency to market their business.

What About Business Brokerage Firms?

The other firms running "Biz Op" ads are business brokerage firms, either independents or local franchise offices. Are they a good bet? The answer is a qualified maybe. There are some excellent business brokerages, or, more accurately, there are some excellent business brokers. There are also some real clunkers. As in any service business, the most important component is the individual who serves you.

You should know that the field is largely unregulated. A few states have some requirements; however, often anyone can hang out a shingle and claim to be in the business. The turnover rate among brokers is much like it is in real estate. In many offices, it's 100 percent. Almost universally, brokers are hired as private contractors and are paid strictly on a commission basis. Often they have no business background whatsoever. And, like real estate agents, they represent the seller's interests, not yours. You can spin your wheels for a long time with brokers who are unlikely to lead you to pay dirt. That's the bad news.

The good news is that there are some gems out there if you're willing to dig. Unlike the brokers you see listed in the Biz Ops, some brokers actually can lead you to good stuff. But you're got to separate the sheep from the goats; otherwise, you can burn a lot of time looking at businesses that are duds or that really don't fit your needs.

The majority of brokers will not be helpful. On the other hand, the really good ones can be extremely helpful.

The very successful brokers have learned that the secret to success is to concentrate on solid, profitable businesses with a history of consistent profit. Too many business brokerage firms take on any business, including many that can only be classified as dogs. But good firms know that although it takes greater effort up front to find good listings, the effort required to sell them is minimal. You won't even see their best listings advertised in the Business Opportunities section. It's just not necessary. Every good broker has a stable of willing buyers waiting for his or her call. Your job should be to identify good brokers and get your name on their priority buyer list (see Chapter 13).

But be realistic. The odds are that you've got less than a 50 percent chance of landing your ideal business through a broker. The numbers are solidly against you. First, although 90 percent of all homes are sold through real estate brokers, fewer than 20 percent of businesses are sold through business brokers. Second, the landscape is crawling with prospective buyers looking for successful small companies. That adds up to a lot of eager buyers competing for a very small number of high-profit companies.

So where does that leave you? Well, it's easy to see why locating a profitable business with a willing seller is such a tough job. You can also see why most people are unsuccessful in their search. The majority of people are searching using Biz Ops and brokers, the two media that are least likely to bring results.

What you need is a way to tap into the market where the high-profit companies are and competing buyers aren't. And you need a way to dramatically improve your odds of finding the business with your name on it. If you can do this, you will have accomplished several objectives, not the least of which is eliminating three-quarters of your competition.

If you've completed the exercises up to this point, you have a clearly defined direction. You know what businesses will fit your skills and interests. You know the size, price range, and geographic limits of what you are after. You also know what you don't want in your business. You have a target. Don't worry that you don't know what specific company fits the bill. If you concentrate on the process created for you in this book and follow it precisely, you'll find it eventually. Your competitors will continue dissipating their energy on the same wild-goose chases with the same lack of results. Unlike them, you'll realize that it's very difficult to catch any goose, let alone the golden goose. You must have a strategy for the chase.

Okay, so how do you tap into that hidden market where your company is waiting? By going directly to the source, bypassing the middlemen and the competition. The techniques and tools you'll use are powerful, yet simple—so simple that you may wonder if they work. They do. They've been used successfully by all kinds of people, many of whom had no special training or background.

8

Let There Be Light

The Secret to Finding Your Business

The starting point in finding the best business for you is research. It's the backbone of your "go direct" strategy for finding and buying a high-profit business. First, it provides the information you need to identify companies that fit your geographic and interest requirements. Second, it provides the marketing and industry data that enable you to make intelligent business decisions about which markets and industries make sense for you.

The first stop is your local library. You'll need a good business reference section, so if your library seems a little lean in this department, you'll have to locate the nearest facility that does have a good business library. Ask your local librarian for help. For those of you who are tapped into on-line services, you can conduct most of your research on the computer.

Research will provide you with the information that you will use to identify prospective companies and to approach the owners directly. In addition, you'll acquire an overall savvy and comprehensive understanding of the industry and business issues that impact the companies you're considering.

Although it's true that the selling price of a business is based on past performance, you'll buy a company on the basis of your judgments about its ability to perform in the future. If you're manufacturing buggy whips, impressive past performance is no assurance of future profits.

Research—What You Need to Know

Your goal in doing research is to gather accurate and timely data. But to be of any use, the research must reflect your assessment of what you need to know in order to make solid decisions. The first thing you'll notice is that your research won't make sense without the insights gained from the exercises in the previous chapters.

Most people buying a business for the first time have no plan, no clear direction, and no understanding of where their skills and interests best fit. Without any idea of what they're looking for, the search deteriorates into a haphazard effort whose outcome has to do more with luck than with skill.

Rather than just hoping that the fates will be kind and help you fall into exactly the right situation, you must analyze your options, determine an appropriate direction, and devise a strategy for attaining your goal.

Your geographic considerations are a good place to start. For some people, residence is unimportant. For many of us, however, where we live is, as we have noted, very important. So, the research you conduct will be driven by your decision about geography. If you've made a family decision to limit your search for a business to within an hour's drive of home, that decision immediately focuses your research.

Let's add even more focus to your research. If you've decided that you've just got to have a company that manufactures Christmas decorations and you really don't care where you live, you'll have many prospective companies to go after. On the other hand, if you wish to continue living in Bangor, Maine, then limiting your search to one industry is very unrealistic.

Many people don't care what industry they're in. What gets their juices flowing is the business side of business. Rocket parts or underwear—it's all the same to them. To others, the industry is everything. The trade-off between geography and industry can be difficult to resolve, but obviously you must make a decision and make it early on in your search. So sit down and give it the attention it needs.

Let's assume you've resolved these two issues. What's next? If you've decided to stay wide open geographically and limit the search to one or two industries, you'll want to start with industry research. If you're considering entering a new industry, you'll want to make sure that you've examined your choice intelligently. Unfortunately, many inexperienced business buyers enter industries that fit neither their talents nor their interests. The result is often a disaster.

How can you avoid this? Be sure you know exactly what you're getting into *before* you make a move. To do that, you need good information from a variety of sources. It's time to hit the books.

Even if you're already in the field, you'll be amazed at how useful industry research will be. If you're not, proceeding without completing industry research is suicide.

If geography is number one, save your industry research until you've identified companies that fit your general interests and are within the boundaries you've defined.

There are many sources of information for conducting your research. You'll be amazed at the breadth and depth of information available. There are literally thousands of directories available, and no one library can inventory all of them. Believe it or not, there's even a directory for all those directories. No matter what the subject, it's likely you'll be able to find a directory.

Here is only a partial list intended to give you an idea of the incredible variety and quantity of directories available. *The Guide to American Directories* and *Directories in Print* list many, many more. Use directories like these to identify specific companies for further investigation:

> *Acoustical Contractors*
> *Advertising-Direct Mail Directory*
> *Air Conditioning Dealers & Contractors*
> *American Association of Exporters & Importers*
> *American Glass Review—Glass Factory Directory*
> *American Society of Landscape Architects Member's Handbook*
> *American Society of Travel Agents*
> *Artificial Flowers, Plants, and Trees Directory*
> *Association of Independent Television Stations*
> *Athletic Business—Buyer's Guide*
> *Automobile Body Shops Directory*
> *Bicycle Dealer Showcase—Buyer's Guide*
> *Bridal Shops Directory*
> *Burglar Alarm Systems Directory*
> *Business Information Sources*
> *Candy Industry Buying Guide*
> *Country Inns of the Southwest*
> *Craft Supply Directory*
> *Directories in Print*
> *Directory of Chain Restaurant Operators*
> *Directory of Door Manufacturers*
> *Directory of Franchising Organizations*
> *Directory of Home Furnishings Retailers*
> *Directory of Mailing List Houses*
> *Directory of Management Consultants*
> *Directory of On-Line Data Bases*

Directory of Publishing
Directory of Truckload Carriers
Directory of U.S. Meat Suppliers
Doughnut Shops Directory
Encyclopedia of Associations
Encyclopedia of Business Information Sources
Gale Directory of Publications & Broadcast Media
Giftwares, Wholesale and Manufacturers
Guide to American Directories
Handbook of Labor Statistics
Hayes Directory of Dental Supply Houses
Industrial and Hazardous Waste Management
Lasers & Optronics Buying Guide
Local Area Networking Sourcebook
Macrae's Industrial Directory—North Carolina, South Carolina, Virginia
Marine Manufacturers
New England Media Directory
Oil & Gas Directory
Pet Shop Directory
Plastics Technology Manufacturing Handbook & Directory
Secondhand Stores
Smoke Signals—Directory of Native Indian/Alaskan Businesses
State & Metropolitan Area Data Book
Statistical Sources
Telephone Equipment & Systems Directory
U.S. Soft Drink Canning, Bottling, and Distributing
Western New England Regional Industrial Buyer's Guide
Wind Energy Directory
World Aviation Directory

Regional directories that profile all manufacturing or service companies by name, city, and industry are especially valuable. *The Directory of New England Manufacturers* is a good example. It lists all manufacturers in New England alphabetically by company name, by city and state, and by product. Under each company listing you'll find the company's address and phone number; the number of employees; the names of key personnel, including the owner; the gross sales for the last year; a description of products; and the Standard Industrial Code (often referred to simply as the SIC Code) that identifies the specific industry.

A typical use for this directory, or one like it, is to locate all the companies in a region that deal in a product of interest to you. If you really gravitate to the furniture business, for example, look up furniture in the product section; you'll find several hundred furniture manufacturers listed.

There are directories for most states that profile both manufacturing and service firms. On the local level, many chambers of commerce and state departments of economic development print excellent directories.

Once you become familiar with the resources, you'll be able to identify nearly every possible company that fits your requirements. Spend the first hour or two in the library just becoming familiar with the business reference section. Get to know the catalog system. Identify relevant directories; learn how they're indexed and what kind of information they provide. And if it's been a while since you've used a library, don't be afraid to ask for help. Librarians are there to serve you. Tell them exactly what you want to know, and they'll help you find it.

Another terrific source of information is trade journals. Trade journals are even more abundant than directories. You'll find a directory of trade journals that will tell you what publications exist in your fields of interest. As an example, consider this partial list for just one industry, the automobile aftermarket.

Aftermarket Business	*Business Driver*
American Carwash Review	*Commercial Carrier Journal*
American Clean Car	*Exhaust News*
Auto Laundry News	*Discount Store News*
Autotrim News	*Fleet Owner*
Automotive Aftermarket News	*Modern Tire Dealer*
Automotive Body Repair	*Professional Carwashing &*
Automotive Cooling Journal	*Detailing*
Automotive Engineering	*Service Station Management*
Body Shop Business	*Specialty Automotive*
Brake & Front End	*Under Car Digest*

Read the industry "trades," as they're called, particularly if you're not already in the field. You'll be amazed at how quickly you'll become an industry expert.

Make absolutely sure you dig out the answers to the following questions:

1. What are the key industry issues?
2. Is the industry growing or dying?

3. Who are the leaders and innovators? Why are they the leaders?
4. What's happened to the industry over the last five years?
5. How is technology affecting the business?
6. Is foreign competition having an impact?
7. What's the potential over the next five years?
8. What's the long-term potential for the industry?
9. What's the size of the industry?
10. What kind of people are in the industry? What kinds of backgrounds do they have?
11. What kind of skills and education are required to work in the industry?
12. How sophisticated is the industry in technology and marketing?
13. What's the mix of large and small companies?
14. Who holds the greatest market share?
15. Can small firms compete effectively?
16. Who's making money, and why?
17. How much on average can a small company do in annual revenue?
18. How much profit can a small firm produce annually?
19. How much capital investment is required to compete effectively?
20. What's the status of international competition?
21. What's the makeup of the employee population in a typical small company?
22. What are the industry problems?
23. How are they being solved?
24. What do the solutions cost?
25. What separates the real performers from the pack?
26. Do my interests fit this industry closely?
27. Do my skills fit?
28. Overall, do my abilities and interests fit better in this industry than any other? Why or why not?

Trade journals are a gold mine. If it's an issue in the industry, you'll find it covered. Study the trades carefully, going back at least three years. Notice the trends and changes. You'll develop an excellent feel for industry, to the point where it becomes easy to say "I love it" or "I hate it."

Trade associations are also an extremely valuable source. They often have extensive data concerning the regulatory environment, markets, and technical issues.

Another excellent resource is *The Business Periodical Index*. Remember those terrible term papers you once had to write? You probably used *The Reader's Guide to Periodical Literature* to identify magazine articles relevant to your topic. *The Business Periodical Index* accomplishes the same purpose for you now. Whatever the business or industry issue, there's a good chance someone has written something about it. Once you've identified an article that's "required" reading, you can go to the periodical section of the library and access it or request a reprint from the publisher.

No matter what your information needs, there are several sources to choose from. In fact, the real problem is staying focused in the face of such a vast amount of information. Here's how to proceed in an organized fashion.

1. Spend an orientation day in the library. Become familiar with how the system works. If you need help, ask your librarian.
2. If you've already decided on an industry to target and you know it intimately, fine. If not, concentrate on industry research.
3. Use directories to identify companies that are possibilities for you. Remember, if you're limiting your search to a specific geographic area, concentrate on the appropriate regional directories. If geography is secondary, focus on the appropriate industry directories.
4. Create a research worksheet like the one shown in Figure 2.
5. Get yourself a large three-ring notebook with alphabetical tabs. Use it to file the company information that you collect. Reserve another section in the notebook for industry research. This simple but remarkably efficient system will save you many hours of trying to remember where you've stashed critical information.

When you're ready to begin your "go direct" campaign, you'll have the names and addresses of the business owners you plan to contact.

Once you've completed the first phase of research, you'll have a long list of good possibilities. Now it's time to winnow the crop. How do you home in on those organizations that you can buy? How do you get connected with sellers who are ready to deal? It's easier than you think.

Figure 2.   Research worksheet.

Name of Company _____

Address _____

Phone _____ President/Owner _____

Industry _____

Products/Services _____

Gross Sales _____ Number of Employees _____

Additional Data

Identifying Your Prospect Companies

At the conclusion of your first round of research, you should have a list of companies, complete with the owner's name, address, and phone number. These are your *suspects.* All you know at this point is that these interesting companies look as if they might be worthy of further consideration. You have no idea if the company is profitable or if the owner has any interest in selling.

Your first goal is to narrow down the list to those whose owner is interested in the possibility of selling. This smaller set of companies is a *prospect* list. Later, after talking with the owner and completing additional research, you'll reduce the *prospect* list to a *candidate* list— those companies that have been qualified still further. These companies have willing sellers, a history of profitability, and a ballpark selling price that's reasonable, and they appear to meet your particular requirements.

Picture it this way: You're using a funnel to target the best business opportunities. You're pouring the *suspects* in at the top, narrowing down to *prospects* who fill the middle of the funnel, and then qualifying still further until the serious contenders, called *candidates,* fall out the bottom.

If this seems much like the process that highly successful busi-ness executives use to identify customers and markets for their products, you're exactly right. They don't wander around aimlessly hoping they'll run into customers. They have a well-designed plan that targets qualified candidates for their products. Every action is calculated, and the results show it.

You may be thinking at this point, "I'm no salesperson! I'm not a strategic planner or a marketing professional. That's just not my field!" Think again. You've been doing these things all your life. You sold your spouse on marrying you. You marketed your talents to a company to get a job. You convinced your kids to accept your values. You developed business strategies for solving important problems for your employer. Obviously, you've done it, and you're pretty good at it. You just didn't think of it as sales, business planning, or marketing. If you're serious about owning your own business, selling, market-ing, and developing good business strategy go with the territory. So don't feel uncomfortable about it. You've been practicing for years.

Contacting Prospective Companies

All right, so now you have a list of prospects. It's time to get in touch with the current owners to see if they're interested in selling.

Your first contact with the prospective business seller is through a personal business letter. Do not deviate from acceptable business decorum in approaching prospective sellers. Although experienced buyers can often telephone prospects directly and make the right impression, we strongly recommend that you "two-step it" with an initial contact letter followed up by a phone call.

The letters should be short, direct, and to the point. They should clearly indicate the next action you will take.

Don't try to get fancy. This is not an opportunity to show off your extensive vocabulary or your creative writing skills. The idea is very straightforward: "I'm interested in the possibility of buying your business. I'm financially and professionally qualified to do so. If you'd like to explore the issue, let's talk. I'll call you to get your answer." That's it. This is a case where less is most definitely more.

The construction of your letter is critical. As in any business situation, packaging is important to convey the right message. When the prospect reads your letter, she should be thinking, "This person is professional, informed, and businesslike. I'd like to meet her." Your letter should demonstrate the results of your research. The more you are seen as a professional who knows the industry, the more credibility you will have.

You need to do two things. First, type your letter on high-quality stationery with absolutely *no* typos. Second, construct a brief but powerful statement of precisely what you want. Remember, the purpose of your letter is to get the owner to say yes to a meeting, not to explain why you want to go into business for yourself. Keep it short, give it punch, and target it to your objective.

Call the company and check the name and address of your prospect. If the receptionist asks you why you want this information, say that you are sending some material to him or her and you just want to verify the address. Don't ever give more information than that. One more thing, and this is important! On the envelope write PERSONAL. You don't want company employees opening your letter.

Figures 3a to 3d should help you construct your own letters.

Figure 3a. Sample letter to business owner.

Ms. Lucy Piper
President
Piper Consulting
237 Winchester Court
St. Louis, MO 92106

Dear Ms. Piper,

I'm an experienced management consultant with broad credentials and long experience. My current objective is to purchase a consulting firm like yours. My initial research indicates that your company may be just what I've been looking for.

I realize you may have no interest in selling. However, if it has ever crossed your mind, it might be worthwhile to explore the possibilities. I'll take the liberty of calling early next week to chat with you.

Cordially,

Charles Ackers

Figure 3b.   Sample letter to business owner.

J. D. Wing
President
SBB Pump Inc.
2 Third Street
Detroit, MI 93215

Dear Mr. Wing,

I've been following the growth of your company for the last few years. You've certainly done well. Currently I'm in the market to buy a business in the pump manufacturing industry.

I've spent twenty-five years in the business, primarily in manufacturing management and sales. Through the grapevine, I've heard of your plans to move to Florida. You've certainly earned the privilege.

I would very much like to sit down with you and explore the possibility of a buyout. I'll be in touch with you in a few days.

Sincerely,

Harold Heath

That First Phone Call

In your letter, you indicate that you'll call to follow up at a specified time. It's important that you do exactly what you said you would do and exactly when you said you would do it. If you don't, your credibility is shot even before you meet.

When the time comes to call prospective sellers, how well you handle the phone may determine whether you get the opportunity to buy the company. Keep in mind that buying a business is not like any other purchase. Strange as it sounds, you must sell the seller on selling. Unless he or she sees the benefits of selling and feels that you're the right buyer, there will be no sale. So you must promote yourself from the very first time you contact the potential seller, until you both ink the deal at the closing.

Figure 3c. Sample letter to business owner.

Mrs. Barbara Donohoe
President
Donohoe Employment Services
18 Harbridge Road
Portsmouth, NH 03801

Dear Mrs. Donohoe,

Your impressive record in the personnel field documents your ability to get things done and to bring innovation to an industry that sorely needs it. Three new offices in less than two years is a terrific track record.

I'm in the market to buy a company like yours. I realize this may be a new idea for you, but if you'd like to explore the possibility, I'd like to meet you and discuss what I have in mind. It could be good for both of us.

I'll call you next week.

Sincerely,

David Morrison

Be certain that you understand the purpose of that first phone call. You've sent an initial contact letter, and now you're following up, just as you said you would. There is only one purpose for your call: to set an appointment to explore the possibility of buying the company. That's it. There's no other purpose. Once that's been accomplished, get off the phone.

Say just enough to convince the seller that it's worthwhile to get together and talk. Don't get into a long discussion that would be much better handled in person. We suggest that you write out what you intend to say. Not that you should use what you've written word for word or, heaven forbid, read it, but you'll feel more comfortable if you've thought through the best way to get what you want—the opportunity to meet with the business owner.

Make sure that you think through in advance the concerns that

Figure 3d.   Sample letter to business owner.

Mark C. Murray
President
WKOL-FM
1890 Sturbridge Street
Boston, MA 02134

Dear Mr. Murray,

Congratulations on the June Arbitrons. I know how tough the Boston market is. After many years in the business on the West Coast, I'm looking to move east and purchase my own station. As I've been conducting my research, your station keeps surfacing as one that fits my interests closely.

I realize this may be a new idea for you. However, I'm interested in designing a deal that you may find worth considering. I'm planning to be in Boston in three weeks. I'll call to see if we can arrange a time to get together.

Sincerely,

Liz Littlefield

---

the owner may bring up and how you'll respond. The owner may flat-out state: "I have no interest in selling and that's final!" Obviously, then it makes little sense to press for a meeting. In many cases, however, if the owner is convinced that it's at least worth talking about, you'll be able to arrange an exploratory meeting. And who knows where it may go from there? The point is that you can't get to second base, third base, and home unless you get to first. So for now, concentrate on getting to first.

The sample dialogues contain several concerns commonly expressed by owners. Draft your responses in your own words. That way, you'll sound sincere, not scripted. Nothing turns people off faster than someone reading from a script.

However, that doesn't grant you the license to wing it. It's a good idea to role-play the initial phone contact until you feel completely comfortable with it. Recruit a close friend or your spouse to help you here. Choose someone who will give you honest feedback and make you practice until you're really ready. That way, you won't blow it on your best candidates.

Above all, remember that the goal of the phone call is to set an appointment. Don't try to conduct business over the phone at this point. You have not established a relationship of trust. In fact, you have no relationship at all. Be warm and friendly, but get the appointment set as quickly as you can, and then get off the phone.

The sample telephone dialogues correspond to the sample letters in Figures 3a through 3d.

Sample Telephone Dialogue 1

You: This is Charles Ackers calling for Lucy Piper.

Receptionist: May I ask why you're calling?

You: Sure. It's a personal call. [*Always say this. First, it is true. It is a personal call. In no way should you consider this a normal business call. And in no way should you discuss your reason for calling with company employees. Second, it always works. No receptionist will ever question you on the nature of your personal call.*]

Owner: This is Lucy Piper.

You: Lucy, Charles Ackers calling. Did you get my letter last week?

Owner: Yes, I did. I must say it took me by surprise.

You: I imagine it did. Have you ever thought about selling?

Owner: No, not seriously.

You: Well, I can certainly understand that. But if the deal were right, would you consider it?

Owner: Maybe, although I'm not sure. The answer is probably no.

You: I'd certainly agree with you that it wouldn't make sense if it weren't a good deal for you. But it wouldn't hurt to talk and see if it's worth pursuing, would it?

Owner: I don't want to waste your time. Why don't I think it over and get back to you?

You: I understand how you feel. I'd feel exactly the same way if I were you. But, look, we're both businesspeople and know that it's usually a good idea to check out an opportunity before making a decision. Why don't we just get together and chat? Maybe it will go somewhere. Maybe it won't.

Owner: I suppose it wouldn't hurt.

You: How's your schedule for next week?

Owner: Tuesday looks okay.

You: That's okay for me, too. How about around ten?

Owner: That will be fine.

You: Great, I'll see you then.

Sample Telephone Dialogue 2

You: I'm calling for J. D. Wing.

Owner: This is J. D. Wing.

You: This is Harold Heath calling. Did you get my letter?

Owner: What letter would that be?

You: I sent you a letter asking whether you'd be interested in talking about selling your business.

Owner: Oh, yes. That letter. Yes sir, most interesting mail I've had in a while.

You: Oh, why's that?

Owner: Well, I'm retiring in the fall and planning to move to Florida. By the way, how'd you find out about that?

You: I've been doing a lot of research and talking to a lot of people in the business. Somebody happened to mention you were heading south. I thought it might make sense to talk with you.

Owner: Maybe.

You: Well, my situation is this. I've worked in the industry for many years. I've got a lot of experience, but I'm thinking about the future. It's time I had my own company and built some equity. The time will come when I'll want to cash out and move to Florida, too, I expect.

Owner: I see. Well, I am interested in selling, but I've got two companies that are interested in buying me out.

You: I don't wonder. You've got an attractive company. People tell me you're the best around. That's why I'm interested in buying. You run a quality outfit that's shown good growth.

Owner: Right. Well, as I said, I've got two live ones already.

You: Well, I understand. But often you can cut a better deal with an individual than you can with a company buying you out. You know how conservative those company accountants can be.

Owner: Hmm.

You: Look, you're in the driver's seat. A lot of companies can't find any buyers. You're in a situation where you can explore all kinds of possibilities. Doesn't it make sense to check out all the options?

Owner: Yeah, it probably does, but I don't know anything about you.

You: That's true. But we can deal with that. Why don't we find a time to get together? I'll give you a complete rundown on my background and what I'm looking for. And you can give me a feel for your business while we explore the possibilities. Who knows, maybe it will turn out to be just what we're both looking for.

Owner: Well, okay. Let's talk.

You: How about Monday morning at eight sharp?

Owner: You got it.

You: See you then.

Sample Telephone Dialogue 3

You: Barbara Donohoe, please.

Owner: This is Barb.

You: Barb, this is David Morrison. I'm calling to follow up my letter of last week.

Owner: Oh, yes. I remember. Thanks for your interest, but I'm not ready to sell yet.

You: Does that mean you've thought about the possibility of selling in the future?

Owner: Hasn't everybody? But I can't afford to retire. I've got to work. If I sold the company, I'd have to work for someone else or go through another start-up. And I don't have the strength for that.

You: Sounds like you've really got your hands full.

Owner: There are days when I wonder why I'm in this business.

You: What if you could sell the business, get rid of the craziness, keep your job with the company, and still make a good living?

Owner: What are you, Santa Claus?

You: Well, I've never been called that, but I do know that it's possible to create business deals where everybody wins. What do you say we talk about it?

Owner: I'm not promising anything other than to listen to what you have to say.

You: That's fair enough. I don't know if it will go anywhere either, but it certainly won't hurt to take a look to see if there's something there. Right?

Owner: Right.

You: You tell me a day that's good for you.

Owner: Wednesday afternoon.

You: How about 2:30?

Owner: Great. See you then.

Sample Telephone Dialogue 4

You: Liz Littlefield calling for Mark Murray.

Receptionist: He's not in. May I take a message?

You: No, when is a good time to call back?

Receptionist: He should be in about ten. You can call his direct line, Ms. Littlefield. He told me to expect your call. The number is 390-2714.

You: Thanks, tell him I'll get to him before noon today.

[Later the same morning]

You: This is Liz Littlefield calling.

Owner: Thanks for calling. I got your letter. I'm sorry to say that the station isn't for sale.

You: Even if the deal were right?

Owner: No. I'm having too much fun and making too much money.

You: Can't I convince you to at least talk about it?

Owner: No way. Just not interested.

You: Well, I'm happy for you. But would you help me out a little? You know the market in the East. If you were me, what stations would you approach?

Owner: Well, I do know people. I've been in the business for a long time. I'd have to think about it a bit.

You: I'd really appreciate any ideas you could give me. Let me call you back, say, the end of the week. That way you'll have time to give it some thought.

Owner: Fair enough.

You: One more thing. As I mentioned in my letter, I'll be in Boston in three weeks. Could we have lunch? Maybe I could pick up some useful information from an old pro like you.

Owner: Love to. Just let me know when, and I'll plan on it.

You: Okay. Let's decide when and where when I call you back later in the week. I'll talk to you then.

A word about the odds. If your experience is typical, you'll have a success rate of 15 to 20 percent. Make twenty contacts, and you'll have four or five meetings lined up with potential sellers. Keep this ratio in mind. It will help you deal with rejection. Rejection is not fun. But just remember, every time you get a no, you're one step closer to a yes. As long as you commit yourself to making the calls, you'll get the yeses in exactly the same ratio as anyone else. Therefore, there's really no excuse for not having as many meetings as you wish. You're in complete control.

If you've completed the exercises up to this point, you've defined the companies that fit your skills, interests, and geographic considerations. You've focused on the specific industries that fit you. You know how to find what's been written about the industry issues in trade journals. You've compiled an extensive list of business owners.

You know how to contact those owners directly and how to set up business meetings to discuss selling.

Not one in ten of your competitors will be using this strategy. It never occurs to most people to forget about going with the herd and instead to go underground, directly to the source. Not only is the direct route easier, it also dramatically increases the odds of uncovering a highly profitable business for which there is virtually no competition!

9

If It Barks Like a Dog

Evaluating a Company's Potential

The time will come in the process of finding and buying your business that you're going to find yourself face-to-face with owners who are quite willing to explore the option of selling their business to you.

Although there will be a number of meetings with the seller, the first personal meeting with the owner of a prospective company is a very important one, with several goals. Certainly, a primary goal is to size up the company as a candidate for purchase. You'll also want to size up the owner so that you'll have some idea of how best to deal with her. Third, you'll want to create the right kind of impression in the mind of the owner. She must like you, respect you, and see you as competent; otherwise, she won't take you seriously.

When you walk out the door at the end of that first meeting, the potential seller will have formed an opinion about you that will drive the decision either to continue talking or to axe further discussion. Remember, this is not the Spanish Inquisition. Of course you want critical information. You also want to leave the impression that you'd be a wonderful person to take over the business. It won't matter how qualified you are to run the business if you're perceived as a class A jerk. Openness, friendliness, honesty, and professionalism are the operative words that should guide your strategy for these meetings.

Always try to arrange the first meeting at the business location. Here are some suggestions on what to be alert for during a meeting with a prospective seller:

1. *Look at the appearance of the facility.* Is it clean, neat, and orderly? Appearances can tell you a good deal about how the business is managed.

2. *Look carefully at the employees.* Do they look happy and busy or depressed and frightened? Morale problems are responsible for serious productivity problems.

3. *If you're given the opportunity to tour the facility, look carefully at raw inventory, work-in-progress, and finished goods.* Later, as you examine the financial statements, you can see if what's claimed is roughly equal to what's really there.

4. *Notice the fixed assets.* Are they old and worn out? Old but well maintained? Does the business have the equipment it needs? If there are problems here, it could you cost plenty.

5. *Notice how often the phone rings.* Busy phones signify a busy business.

6. *Take the initiative with openness.* If you're willing to give information freely about yourself and your goals, the owner will begin to trust you and provide the inside information you need about the company.

7. *Get the owner to discuss customers.* You want to know how many, revenue per customer, amount of repeat business, and how business is generated. A steady flow of business from a solid customer base is the single most important dimension of a business.

8. *Analyze the owner's personality and style.* How does he make decisions? What's important to him? What are his plans? This is critical information when it comes time to construct a deal that will be attractive.

9. *Pay attention to gut feeling.* It's telling you something.

10. *Before you leave, make sure you both agree on what the next step should be and the timing for that step.*

There is a lot to do in that first meeting. And although part of this analysis will be done when you meet the owner for the first time, the bulk will occur after that meeting. There are literally hundreds of questions to be answered. Financial, tax, and legal considerations are critical. To ignore them could be disastrous.

First Things First: Establishing Rapport and Building Trust

So you've set up a first meeting with the business owner. Remember, the purpose of that meeting is to gather enough information to assess the company as a prospect and to build trust and rapport between yourself and the owner. After all, if the owner doesn't like you or trust you, you're unlikely to get information of any value.

Whatever you do, don't underestimate the importance of building trust and rapport. Would you reveal any meaningful information about a business you owned to a perfect stranger? Of course not. It takes a while to get comfortable enough to relax and share information. So begin the meeting by addressing the primary concern of all business owners: confidentiality. You must be certain to allay the owner's fear of a breach of confidence through a nondisclosure agreement.

A sample nondisclosure agreement is shown in Figure 4. Be sure to bring one to your first meeting with a seller. In it, you promise not to reveal any information about the business to anyone else without the express permission of the owner. Most business owners will have far less resistance to handing over confidential information if they feel that you'll be discreet. The use of a nondisclosure agreement identifies you as a trustworthy business professional who understands and respects these concerns. Here's how to deal with this issue.

1. Use the sample nondisclosure agreement shown in Figure 4 to create your own. Prepare copies, and have them available whenever you meet with a business owner.

2. Early in your first meeting with the owner, emphasize your commitment to protecting his privacy. Indicate that everything that he tells you, along with any written records you are given, will be treated with complete confidentiality. When it's necessary to share information with your advisers, promise you'll get his prior approval.

3. After you have explained your commitment to confidentiality, take out two copies of your nondisclosure agreement. Tell the owner what they are, fill them out, and sign them. Ask the owner to sign them also. Keep one copy for your records, and leave one copy with the owner. And then make sure that you do what you promised: Maintain the owner's confidentiality. Breach of contract could prove costly.

The building of trust and rapport goes beyond the signing of a nondisclosure agreement, however. At this point, limit your discussion to broad issues that will not be threatening. Start by summarizing your background, and explain how you arrived at the decision to contact the owner. Now is the time to produce the Business Background Summary that you completed in Chapter 5. The fact that you

Figure 4.   Nondisclosure agreement.

Name of Business _____

Address _____

As a prospective buyer of the above-named business, I acknowledge receipt of personal and confidential information. I agree not to divulge such information to others, except to secure their advice and counsel, in which case I agree to obtain their commitment to the same confidentiality.

I further agree not to contact other owners, customers, suppliers, or employees regarding the business or business affairs of the above-named business without the knowledge and consent of the owner.

Date _____

Name _____

Address _____

_____

Signature _____

Owner Signature _____

are direct and friendly and that you are so willing to share the details of your background will go a long way toward creating an atmosphere of openness and trust.

You should then move the meeting along by asking the owner to talk about himself; ask how he came to be in this business. Ask him to share his background and to tell you how that experience helped or hindered him in managing the company.

First-Pass Analysis: What to Look For

Since people love to talk about themselves, asking the owner to talk about his business experiences is an excellent icebreaker, as well as a natural bridge to a discussion about the business. You'll want answers to such questions as: What business are you in? What are the products and services? If this seems too basic, you must remember that many business owners have given little thought to these fundamental questions. An owner may believe he's in the burglar alarm business, when he should be positioning his company in the corporate security business. This is far from a subtle distinction. Positioning the company to sell and service burglar alarms limits the services and products that can be marketed. On the other hand, suppose the owner starts to think of his business as a provider of corporate security services. Consider the possibilities: prevention of employee theft; fire protection; data protection; off-site storage of vital records; authorized access control; remote monitoring of heating, air-conditioning, and electric power; air and water quality monitoring; and on and on.

The point for you is this: The more problems you can solve for each customer, the more value your company has and the more revenue you'll generate. The company you're looking at may have tremendous potential that the current owner just doesn't see.

Defining a clear vision of a company's mission and developing a solid strategy to provide answers for customers' problems is no small task. However, poor performance is often directly related to muddy thinking about the definition of the business. If you're able to see untapped potential, redefine the business, and develop a plan for expanding the product line and developing new services, then you may have found a great little company.

You can use the Business Profile Worksheet in this chapter to collect and organize important business information about the company you're considering. Use it as a guide to your interview with the business owner. Ask the owner if she minds if you jot down a few things as you chat. Most owners will have no objection. Then take extensive notes. You can't possibly remember everything that's important without a written record. Later, you'll be able to compare what the owner has told you with your personal research. Once you prime the pump and get things flowing, you'll find that most owners will tell you everything. They just can't help themselves. Here are a few things to keep in mind as you collect the data.

For question 1, on the company's history, be sure to record a complete history. You'll want to capture such things as who started the company, where, and why; how long the company has existed; ownership changes; growth and expansion details; key events, both positive and negative; location changes; and any addition of key

(Text continues on p. 110.)

BUSINESS PROFILE WORKSHEET

Name of business _____

Address _____

Owner(s) _____

Phone _____

1. History from start-up to present.

   _____

   _____

2. Products and services:
   • What types are offered? _____

   _____

   • What is the mix of products and/or services? _____

   _____

3. Geographic market:
   • How is the location? _____

   _____

   • What are the demographics? _____

   _____

4. Number of years in business:
   • Were there periods of expansion? When? _____

   _____

   • Are there any branch offices? _____

   _____

   • Are there any other locations? _____

   _____

5. Reason(s) for selling:
   • Why did the owner originally buy or start the business? _____

   _____

6. Industry maturity:
   • Is the industry embryonic, emerging, or mature? _____

   _____

7. Revenue over the last five years:
   • Make sure you get copies of the financials—balance sheets, profit-and-loss statements, tax returns. _____

   _____

8. Profit for the last five years:
   • Are there hidden expenses? _____ _____ _____

   _____

   • Actual owner benefit (i.e., the total of the owner's salary, benefits, all perks and profit. See chapter 11 for a detailed discussion of owner benefit analysis.): _____

   _____

9. Employees:
   • How many are there? Full-time? Part-time? _____

   _____

   • Are there key employees? _____

   _____

   • What has the turnover rate been? _____

   _____

   • Get a list of all employees, including job descriptions, length of service, wages, and benefits. _____

   _____

(continues)

10. Key vendors:
    • Who are they? _____

    _____

    • How long have they been doing business with this company?

    _____

    _____

    • What are the terms of credit, and are they likely to change?

    _____

    _____

11. Pending litigation, licensing difficulties, or patent problems.

    _____

    _____

12. Lawsuits in the last five years:
    • What were they? _____

    _____

    • Who filed them and why? _____

    _____

    • What was the disposition of each? _____

    _____

13. Local zoning:
    • Are there any zoning problems? _____

    _____

    • Are zoning changes likely in the near future? _____

    _____

    • Are there parking problems? _____

    _____

• What are the regulations regarding signage? _____

_____

14. Copyrights, patents, databases, customer lists, mailing lists, or other proprietary information that the business depends on.

_____

_____

15. Inventory:
    • What is the total dollar value? _____

    _____

    • How much is raw inventory, work-in-progress, finished goods?

    _____

    • What is the value of each type of inventory? _____

    _____

    • How many times does the inventory turn over each year?

    _____

    _____

16. Accounts receivable and accounts payable:
    • What is the total amount of each? _____

    _____

    • What portion of the A/R is overdue 30 days? 60? 90? More than 90 days? _____

    _____

    • What is the bad-debt history? _____

    _____

    • What is the billing/pay cycle?

    _____

(continues)

17. Assets:
    - What is the fair market value for each asset? Get a list for each category.
        - Furniture? _____
        - Fixtures? _____
        - Equipment? _____
        - Vehicles? _____
        - Leases? _____
        - Other assets? _____

18. Lease for real estate (get a copy of the lease):
    - What is the monthly rent? _____

    _____

    - Is this likely to change? _____

    _____

    - What is the duration of the lease? _____

    _____

    - Is it assignable? _____

    _____

    - What are the options and the restrictions? _____

    _____

    - Are there additional payments for taxes, insurance, maintenance?

    _____

    _____

19. Other leased equipment:
    - Is there any other leased equipment? _____

    _____

    - What are the terms? _____

    _____

• Is the lease assignable? _____

_____

20. Customer profile:
    • Are there key customers? _____

_____

    • How long have they been customers? _____

_____

    • What is the total number of customers? _____

_____

    • What is the revenue per customer? _____

_____

    • What is the percentage of repeat business? _____

_____

21. Items and equipment not included in the sale of the business:
    • Get a complete list. _____

_____

22. Advertising:
    • How is the advertising handled? _____

_____

    • What is the budget? _____

_____

    • Where is advertising placed? _____

_____

    • What is the frequency? _____

_____

(continues)

- Are the results tracked? If so, how? _____

  _____

- Get copies of ads. _____

  _____

23. Sales and marketing:
    - What is the strategy? _____

      _____

    - What are the sales projections for the next two years?

      _____

      _____

    - How were they derived? _____

      _____

    - What sales and marketing promotions are used? _____

      _____

    - Do sales and marketing reps attend trade shows? Results?

      _____

      _____

    - Who is responsible for sales? _____

      _____

    - What percentage of the owner's time is spent on sales?

      _____

      _____

    - What percentage of the total sales does the owner generate?

      _____

      _____

24. Competitors:
    • Who is the competition? _____
    _____

    • Do they operate differently? _____
    _____

    • Do they have a competitive advantage? _____
    _____

    • If so, what is it? _____
    _____

    • Where are they located? _____
    _____

    • What is their market share? _____
    _____

    • What is the size of the total market? _____
    _____

25. Market position:
    • How does this company position itself in the market? _____
    _____

    • What is the company's reputation in the marketplace?
    _____

    • What image does the company project? _____
    _____

    • Why and how? _____
    _____

    • Is it a low- or high-cost provider? _____
    _____

(continues)

• Is it a technological leader? _____

_____

• Is it a turnkey provider? _____

_____

• Is it a high-service provider? _____

_____

• Is its product high- or low-quality? _____

_____

• Is the product noncompetitive? _____

_____

26. Key business strengths.

_____

_____

27. Key business weaknesses.

_____

_____

28. Potential for add-on products and services.

_____

_____

29. Merger/acquisition potential.

_____

_____

30. Outside factors that may influence the business positively or negatively.

_____

_____

31. Current market niche:
    • Will it remain stable? _____

    _____

    • Are there untapped markets? _____

    _____

32. Separate operations or divisions.

    _____

    _____

33. Distributors:
    • Who are they? _____

    _____

    • Where are they? _____

    _____

    • What is the business arrangement? _____

    _____

    • What percentage of sales are they responsible for? _____

    _____

    • How much time and money is spent servicing distributors? _____

    _____

    _____

34. Rework/avoidable costs:
    • What are the totals? _____

    _____

    • How are they determined and tracked? _____

    _____

    • What is the figure for scrap? _____

    _____

(continues)

• Are there discounts and customer allowances? _____

_____

• What are the amounts? _____

_____

• How do all these figures compare to industry norms? _____

_____

35. Entry barriers:
    • What is the cost to enter the industry? _____

    _____

    • What technical knowledge and experience are required?

    _____

    _____

    • How much time does it take to break in? _____

    _____

36. Recent growth or change.

    _____

    _____

37. Importance of the current owner to the success of the business.

    _____

    _____

---

employees. As the details get filled in, you'll begin to get a picture of the market the business plays in, its financial performance, and its management capability. You'll notice that a number of later questions pick up critical information in case you missed it in question number 1.

Question 7, on revenue over the last five years, means exactly that—five years. One year doesn't mean much. Get the same information for profit. Make sure your figures are accurate. You'll then be able to see the revenue trend over time and whether profitability has been consistent. The best indicator of future performance is past performance. If the company has no record of growth or consistent profitability, is it likely to do any better with you at its head?

Pay attention to question 9, dealing with employee history and current status. Employee data often tell an interesting story. Look for signs of good and bad management (turnover and low pay). Divide gross revenue by the number of employees to get the revenue per employee. Divide profits by the number of employees to get profitability per employee. These figures can then be used to compare productivity with other companies in the same industry.

When you collect data about customers in question 21, pay attention to how the revenue is distributed. If the lion's share is from only a few customers, ask what would happen if the company lost one or two of them? Find out how long key customers have been with the company and why.

Because every situation is unique, you'll want to add additional questions that apply in your particular case.

The last question on the worksheet is perhaps the most important. In many small, closely held companies, the owner is the business. Often the bulk of the revenue is directly related to the owner's personal relationships with customers. It's not unusual for business volume to decrease drastically when a business changes hands. And when the owner, along with his special talents, leaves, where will that leave you?

The information you collect on the worksheet should be the basis for discussion with your professional advisers. It will provide them with a detailed picture of the business that will enable them to generate a list of additional questions that need answers.

At some point the owner may ask if you'd like a tour. In fact, if you've been successful in establishing rapport, this is quite common. People love to show off their babies. If it happens, terrific! If not, don't push. You can always cover that in a second meeting. Just remember that this situation is no different from any other relationship-building situation. Some people move quickly, some don't. Use your best judgment. In any event, don't bulldoze your way toward your objective! Go only as fast as the situation warrants.

First meetings typically last three to five hours. Don't push for longer. You'll both be tired, and you'll start to miss valuable information. If the meeting lasts only a couple of hours, that's okay. Be sensitive to where the owner is, and wind it up when you sense she's ready for it to end.

A Full Business Workup: What and How

Now that you have valuable information about the business from the owner, you can use it as the foundation for a full workup on the company—financial analysis, market survey, and industry assessment. It's easier than you think.

First, remember the discussion on industry research in Chapter 8? Now that you have a specific company to evaluate within an industry, go back to the library. What you want to know is: Where does this particular company fit into the industry? Is it a leader or a follower? How does its performance compare to industry standards? Who are the local competitors? What is its market share? How does the quality of its products compare? Is its technology up to date? What is its competitive edge? Is it growing faster or more slowly than its competitors?

What you're trying to do is benchmark this company, to give it a report card. In a short time, you'll have figured out what industry leaders are doing that makes them winners and be able to use that information as a yardstick for measuring your target company.

As part of your investigative process, you must talk with both customers and competitors. The old saying "If you want the truth, go straight to the horse's mouth" applies here. Although sellers will have justifiable concerns about letting you talk to customers and competitors, there is a way to handle it so that no damage results to the company. Explain your approach to the seller so that he feels comfortable. If he absolutely refuses to let you call customers, he'd better have excellent reasons. Usually the problem is either that there's something to hide or that you haven't sold him on your approach to the point that he trusts you to pull off the contact without negative consequences.

Meeting the Competitors

When you're choosing which competitors to meet with, select them from a noncompeting geographic area where there's less chance that the competitor will fear that you'll use the information you obtain to take away customers.

Then call the competitors. You can take either of two approaches here. One approach is to indicate that you are thinking about buying a company in this field and would like to get some information about the industry to help you make a decision; you feel that the best information would come directly from professionals experienced in the business; thus your call. Would you respond positively to such a call? Of course you would. Most people love to help if they're approached properly.

The second approach is to say to the competitor that you're doing research about this industry and would like to tap her experience and get her opinion about the state of the industry.

Once you've received a go-ahead for the interview, ask these basic questions:

1. Who are the major players in the industry?
2. Who are the best companies in the industry? Why?
3. What is the market size?
4. What are the untapped markets?
5. What changes are occurring in the industry? How are those changes impacting the business?
6. What do you have to do in order to make money in the industry?
7. What are the industry problems?
8. What kind of background is needed to get into this business?
9. What will the industry be like five years from now?
10. What is the best way to increase market share?
11. How do you keep overhead down?
12. How much time and money should be devoted to R&D?
13. What is the best selling strategy?
14. What are the key concerns of customers?
15. How important is price in this industry?

By asking all these questions, you're getting an MBA in how to manage successfully the company you're thinking about buying. And you're getting it from seasoned, successful professionals who make their living from the information they're sharing with you. Getting smart is a matter of knowing who to ask and what to ask. In a short time you'll know more about the industry than many people who've been in it for years. You'll also know volumes about your target company.

Interviewing Customers

Now it's time to gather information from the most important source of all—the customers. Customers buy products and services for many reasons. You need to know those reasons and why they buy from the company you're considering making your own.

Your approach to interviewing customers should be pretty much the same as the approach you took with competitors. You have a good idea of who the customers are. Most likely, they'll be flattered that you asked for their input. For many, it's the first time they've ever been asked about their motivation for buying or their level of satisfaction with a product or service.

Ask the seller to provide a cross-section of customers—satisfied customers, as well as ones who will provide less-than-glowing reports. You need to know both the good and the bad.

Plan to talk with customers after most of your research has been completed. Your research will have uncovered the key issues and concerns that customers can help you with. If you talk with them too soon, your questions won't be focused because you won't be sure what you need to know.

There's no need to tell customers that you're considering a buyout. A better approach is to tell them that you're doing research for the company to help it improve and that information directly from customers is part of the strategy to create a plan for that improvement.

The questions you ask should be driven by the decisions you want to make. Is there really a market here? How well is it being served? What customer needs are not being met? How much can the market be expanded? Are there opportunities for greater margins? Is there an opportunity to develop new products and services for the same customer base?

Specific Questions to Ask Customers

1. How long have you been a customer?
2. Why do you do business with the company?
3. What was your best experience with this company?
4. What about the worst?
5. How does the quality of the product or service compare with the quality of the competition's?
6. How well does the product or service meet your requirements?
7. What specific improvements are needed?
8. How much business will you write with the company this year?
9. What would convince you to give the company more business?
10. What must the company do to keep your business?
11. How should the products or services be priced?

12. What's important to you about the product? What's not important?
13. What would cause you to switch suppliers?

Customers are the lifeblood of any business. Your business will prosper only if you're able to meet the rapidly changing requirements of those customers. Most people who place their life savings on the line to buy a business never bother to seek out customers and to listen very, very carefully to what they have to say. Since your customer base will be far and away your most important business asset, don't shortcut this part of your analysis.

When and How to Meet Employees

Before you actually sign on the dotted line and become a business owner, you should meet and talk at length with key employeees. After all, if everything goes well, soon they'll be your employees. This is often an extremely delicate matter, and most sellers don't want to tip their hand with employees until they're sure the sale is actually going to happen. If the deal falls through for some reason, the seller is the one who will be required to pick up the pieces and move on. On the other hand, if there are potential employee problems, you must resolve them before you buy.

Usually buyers and sellers agree to employee interviews as one of the very last contingencies before closing the deal. Here's how to approach your chat with employees.

1. *Determine the key employees that you wish to interview.* If the company is very small, you may want to talk with everyone. The current owner should inform the employees at the appropriate time that she's seriously considering selling the business to you. As part of the investigative process, you'll be talking with them to get their views on the business.

Timing is critical here. Work out a schedule acceptable to the seller that leaves as little time as possible between when she drops the bombshell and when you conduct your interviews. The rumor mill can do a lot of damage. Also, make sure that you meet employees one-on-one, without the current owner. You'll have better odds that they will level with you.

2. *Prepare carefully for these meetings.* Job one is to reassure employees. Think how you would feel if this were happening to you.

There's bound to be stress and a great deal of concern about what's going to happen.

Typically employees have these questions: Will I get fired? Will I have to perform a different job? Will I be able to get along with the new owner? Will I still have input into decisions? What changes will take place, and how will they affect me?

While being completely honest, do everything you can to assure employees that things will be fine. Tell them about your background and what you bring to the business.

3. *Explain your management philosophy.* We're not talking concept and theory here. We're talking nitty-gritty. That means telling employees specifically how you as the boss will work with them on a day-to-day basis. Ask for their observations about the strengths and weaknesses of the company, and make sure that they believe you when you say you want their input.

4. *Then ask them about their concerns.* Find out what's worrying them, and deal with it on the spot if possible. But don't make promises you can't keep. It's best to underpromise and overdeliver. Simply say that you're committed to a fair and open atmosphere and that you'll do everything possible to ensure that the company is a great place to work.

5. *Be on the alert for any problems that might change your feelings about the purchase.* If, for example, the manufacturing manager or the sales manager decides to take a hike when the business is sold, you're in deep trouble. Even worse, he may agree to stay but hold you hostage for a raise the company can't afford. Identify attitude problems if possible. It's often hard to do that in one meeting, but if you're going to have problem employees, you'd better do everything you can to isolate and deal with them early. If the problems are serious, you may decide you just don't want those workers.

6. *Get a good feel for employee morale and for any underlying issues that could have an impact on the business after the sale.* Ask employees to level with you just as you did with them. They know better than anyone else where the sore spots are in the organization. Ask what they like and what they don't like about the company. Ask what they'd like to see changed and why. Ask how the company could be managed more profitably.

You may find it difficult to believe, but as long as you assure employees that you really do want their ideas and that anything they say is for your ears only, you'll usually get excellent information. A good way to do this is to get key employees off their turf. Take them to lunch, and make it leisurely. It works one-on-one or with as many as three employees, as long as they are all at the same level. Never take a boss and her subordinate to lunch. All you'll get is what the subordinate is willing for his boss to hear.

If you can produce reasonably accurate data in all these areas, it will be easy for you to make a judgment about the future prospects of the company you are considering.

The majority of business buyers have great difficulty making a sound decision whether to buy a particular business. The problem usually boils down to lack of meaningful data. If you have the right information and know how to interpret it, the decision is simple. The sad truth is that many buyers spend less time picking out a business than they do picking out a Christmas tree.

If you have diligently plowed through the data collection and analysis, you're going to be in great shape for making an intelligent buying decision based on facts and data, not opinion and blind hope—a decision that takes into account both your personal require-ments and the realities of the business you're evaluating. In Chapter 10, we look closely at what financial data can disclose about the current health and future potential of any company you may be considering.

10

Pretend and Lie

What Financial Records Can and Can't Tell You

At the end of the first session with your potential seller, you should have a reasonably good understanding of the business. But there's still one very important and delicate issue to address—the financials.

Much as a biography profiles a person's life, the financials of a business tell an interesting story about the business's ups and downs. To a large extent, finance is the language of business. For those who speak the language, there's a rich history from which intelligent judgments can be made concerning the company's future. You certainly want to have this information before you make a decision to buy.

Although the financials are a written record of a company's success or failure, that's only the beginning. For those who can interpret what the numbers are saying, there's also a clear record of the owner's business decisions, his management competence, and his expertise in key functional areas, such as sales, marketing, operations, and finance.

Perhaps most important of all, you can have absolutely no idea what a business is worth without access to its financial history. With the help of your accountant, you need to run a financial analysis on the company to help you establish a ballpark purchase price.

So, if possible, you'll want to leave your first meeting with copies of the financials for at least the last three years. Financial records covering the last five years would be better still. How quickly a business owner will fork over such intimate details about his business will depend on his personal style. Some people are highly sensitive about their financial life. Some are not. Other factors are how he feels about you and how interested he is in selling. Do ask what is required of you in order to get the financials. You can't proceed much further without them.

If you manage in the first meeting to get answers to your questions about the company and come away with financial records, congratulations. If you've agreed to meet again and have even agreed on an agenda for that second meeting, you've done well indeed. Now, however, the real work begins.

Although you've already logged a good deal of research time, your financial analysis is the single most critical factor in determining a go or no-go decision. There are two goals. The first goal is to decipher the actual history of the company's performance. The second is to price the business. Without complete and accurate financials, it's impossible to do either.

A word of caution: What you'll learn about financial analysis and valuation here will not replace your need for a good accountant. Although the major factors your accountant will be looking for are quite predictable, every case has unique twists that can prove disastrous if not analyzed with an experienced eye.

Here's an example. You've found a great company. It fits your background perfectly. Best of all, the last two years have been especially profitable. You decide, "Wow, this is it!" Fortunately, you have a good accountant who examines your prospective pride and joy and discovers the following: The owner has been using up inventory without replacing it for the last eighteen months. She owns the building and currently pays herself only half the rent you'd be required to pay after you buy the business. Twenty percent of the company's revenue was from the sale of company assets over the last two years. Her sister-in-law is a CPA and takes care of the company's accounting needs gratis. Her husband works full-time in the business without pay. And the company's fixed assets are now fully depreciated. Since the seller insists on a stock sale, you completely lose the cash flow that a depreciation allowance provides.

Suddenly, your highly profitable business doesn't look as attractive. In fact, your accountant figures that if you buy the business, you'll be looking at a substantial loss for several years.

Although this book won't make you a financial expert, at least you won't be completely green. The goal here is to give you what you need to read between the lines and to help you both develop an accurate picture of your target company's financial performance and set a preliminary purchase price. Whatever you do, don't tune out here! You may not think of yourself as a financial person, but owning and managing a successful business requires a working knowledge of finance. And if you're ever to make a smart decision about what company to buy and what to pay for it, you've got to grit your teeth and learn the basics.

First, what kind of financial records do you need? The two primary ones are a statement of financial position, called a balance sheet, and an income statement, often called a profit and loss statement. If the business is a corporation, the company's accountant prepares these documents at the end of each fiscal year. Even if the company is not a corporation, most business owners still have them prepared.

In cases where these documents are not available, proceed with extreme caution. You'll need special assistance from your financial adviser. You should also request the company's tax returns. This is an excellent way to verify financial statements. Any reluctance on the part of the seller to provide tax documents is an indication of serious problems. The data you have may well be false. Do not go ahead with a business purchase unless, as a contingency, the seller agrees to release tax returns to you at some point before the deal is final.

The Balance Sheet: A Snapshot in Time

A balance sheet is very much like a snapshot. It's a picture taken at a particular point in time and profiles the company's assets, liabilities, and the owner's equity. It's expressed as of a particular date, usually the end of the fiscal year. Most small businesses use the calendar year as the fiscal year; however, choosing another date often makes things easier and less expensive. For example, if a company's shipments are highly seasonal, the low point in the inventory cycle would be a logical point to end the fiscal year because the time required to count inventory is minimal.

Essentially, the balance sheet illustrates a fundamental accounting equation: Assets = Liabilities + Stockholder's Equity.

The first half of the balance sheet records the company's assets. The second half lists the liabilities and the stockholder's equity. Notice the analogy to a child's seesaw, thus the term balance sheet.

Refer to the following examples of balance sheets. Under assets you'll notice several subgroups. The subgroup listed as current assets (also called short-term assets) refers to cash on hand and to assets that can be converted to cash within one year.

There are also subgroups under liabilities. The first subgroup, balancing current assets, is current liabilities. Current liabilities are short-term debts that must be paid within one year. Two common examples of current liabilities are accounts payable and bank lines of credit.

The difference between current assets and current liabilities gives you a picture of the company's cash position, or liquidity. This is the working capital that every company needs to manage cash flow effectively. It literally makes the difference between success and failure. A company without enough liquidity does not have enough cash to pay its bills and is in deep trouble.

Smart business owners, however, keep actual cash to an absolute minimum, putting the excess into short-term investments that earn interest. Cash just sitting in the company checking account is not making money for the company.

After cash and short-term investments, the next most liquid asset is the accounts receivable. Accounts receivable are also considered current assets. When you look at your target company's balance sheet, add the following: cash, short-term investments, and accounts receivable. That sum is what accountants call quick assets. Quick assets can be converted into cash relatively fast. They are another indicator of a company's financial health.

Often it's more useful to express the quick assets as a ratio, called a Quick Ratio. By using a ratio, you can compare your target company with the industry average. To get the Quick Ratio, divide the most liquid assets (that is, cash, short-term securities, and accounts receivable) by the current liabilities. The rule of thumb is that a ratio of 1 to 1 is the acceptable minimum, but we suggest that you aim for 2 to 1 to give yourself a good cushion. Since business life is unpredictable, a company with the ability to raise cash in a hurry can more readily weather the inevitable storms that may hit any business from time to time.

Now divide the total of current assets by the total of current liabilities. The resulting number is called the Current Ratio. This is a measure of the company's liquidity, or, in other words, its ability to meet short-term obligations. A ratio above 2 to 1 is considered strong. If the number is negative, watch out! There may be some exceptions to this, which your accountant can point out. But generally, the Current Ratio tells you a great deal about the financial strength.

Keep in mind that all this talk about liquidity is not idle chatter or a pointless, abstract exercise. Small companies simply can't afford to make big mistakes and just write them off. Failure to control liquidity can bring on bankruptcy in a flash.

Long-term assets are those holdings that would take more than one year to convert into cash. They, like short-term assets, are broken down into subgroups. Long-term assets are fixed assets, such as furniture, fixtures, equipment, and real estate, as well as securities held as long-term investments. Occasionally you may also find intangible assets listed on the balance sheet.

Long-term liabilities are the total company debt that is due more than one year from the date of the balance sheet. You may be surprised to find stockholders' equity listed as a liability. But it is listed that way because it reflects what the owner has invested in the company. In most privately held companies, the stockholders' equity is the retained earnings that were left in the company to help it grow or, in some cases, to survive. It really can be viewed as a debt the company owes to the stockholders.

So a balance sheet can tell you a great deal about your target company. It can tell you if the company has enough cash to run the business, what the assets are, and how the assets compare to the liabilities.

Don't be surprised to find that many companies are so highly leveraged that they actually have a negative net worth. If the company has substantial assets to borrow against, that could help you a great deal when it comes time to structure a debt package that will enable you to buy the company. If all the assets are already leveraged, there's nothing to borrow against, and it's often tough to find a way to buy unless you have substantial cash. The balance sheet quickly tells you how much unused debt capacity is available.

And the balance sheet tells you even more. Once you have a basic understanding of what information is found here and why, you'll be able to understand what your accountant is telling you about the health of your target company. Study the sample balance sheets until you understand what each entry means on both the asset and the liability sides.

The Income Statement: Where Money Comes From and Where It Goes

The income, or profit and loss, statement compares the company's revenue to its costs. Revenue is simply the money received from customers, investments, and any other source that generates income. Costs or expenses are the price paid to do business. Unlike the balance sheet, which is a snapshot of the company's financial position at a particular point in time, the income statement gives a picture of what has happened over a period of time, such as a month, a quarter, or a year.

Like the balance sheet, the income statement tells quite a story. Look at the examples included here. The income statement begins by listing all sources of revenue or income. The next entry on the income statement is a breakdown of the cost of goods or materials required to do business. When the cost of goods is subtracted from the revenue, the result is listed as the gross profit.

Next is a line item rendering of what are called operating expenses. You're going to find this section very interesting reading for every company you consider buying. The operating expenses tell you what is happening to most of the cash generated by the business. How is the owner disbursing funds? What are the major costs of doing business in this company? Are those costs increasing every year? Is the company fat in some of its operating costs? For example, are there too many employees with wages that are too high? When you study the income statement, it's often quite easy to see opportunities for pumping up the bottom line by reducing operating costs.

You'll also be able to see why the company may have been having problems. For example, if gross revenue seems lower than it should be and the expense listed for advertising is extremely low for this type of business, there just may be a cause-and-effect relationship here. If freight costs seem high, it may be because the company can't seem to ship on time and must use the expensive service of overnight delivery to get products to customers. Even worse, the freight costs may be unusually high because customers are refusing to accept shoddy merchandise and are returning it, requiring it to be reshipped at a later date.

Look at the rent figure. Does it seem higher than it needs to be for this kind of operation? Scrutinize each line item to see if it makes sense. Not only must you be able to read each line, you must be able to read between the lines as well. Why? Because often the line items in the operating expenses don't mean exactly what they say.

Small business owners, like all of us, want to reduce their tax obligation. Therefore they try to do everything possible to reduce taxable income. That huge travel cost under operating expenses may be airline tickets to grandmother's house or "business" trips to Florida in February. The $12,000 transportation expense may be the lease payments on the owner's new Jag. And the $40,000 salary for the executive vice president may pay a spouse who shows up twice a month.

Many business owners are straight arrows. They wouldn't dream of running personal expenses through the business. Many others have a more liberal approach. The point is simply that a business that appears to be producing only a modest profit may, in fact, be producing a very high profit. It's just not visible unless you know where to look.

There are still a couple of additional items that should interest you about the income statement. First and foremost is the net profit. Net profit is what's left over after the total of the operating expenses and the cost of goods is subtracted from the revenue. Net profit as a percentage of net sales is called the profit margin. This is an extremely important figure. The acceptable range for this margin varies considerably from industry to industry; however, the median for all companies is roughly 5 percent.

If your target company has a higher profit margin than others in the same business, great. If it's lower, you'll want to investigate the reasons. Excellent margins mean the company can withstand business downturns—and can make the owner richer, of course. If the profit margin is very low, a couple of percentage points can make the difference between operating at a loss and operating profitably.

Don't be distracted by the various terms used to express the same thing on both the balance sheet and the income statement. Gross sales and revenue are used interchangeably. An income statement is the same as a profit and loss statement. After you've had an opportunity to study a few financial reports, you'll feel at home with whatever terminology is used.

Interpreting the Financials

Study the financial records in Figures 5 and 6. Then, when you review documents from an actual prospective company, the formats will seem familiar.

The two examples here are from very different companies. In Figure 5A, the company balance sheet shows current liabilities exceeding current assets. Remember to watch out for this situation! It may well indicate that a company is in trouble.

Yet if you look at the income statement, you'll see that the company ended the year with a fine profit picture. How can this be? The explanation is simple. The firm is a highly seasonal manufacturing business. All of the sales take place in the first quarter. All revenue comes in during the last quarter. Note the large interest expense of $150,000 on the income statement. That interest pays for a line of credit that, in turn, pays operating expenses for nearly the entire year. So things are not always what they seem. This is just one example of why you need to work closely with your accountant.

The company in Figure 6 is a very small service company. It's a

Figure 5a. Balance sheet for Company A.

BALANCE SHEET
YEAR ENDING DECEMBER 31, 19_____

ASSETS

Current Assets

Cash	$ 2,000
Accounts receivable	17,500
Inventory	312,000
Due from officers	200,500
Total current assets	532,000

Equipment

Leasehold improvements	24,500
Auto	45,000
Equipment	250,000
Less: Accumulated depreciation	(150,000)
Net property & equipment	169,500

Other Assets

Real estate	375,000
Total Assets	$1,076,500

LIABILITIES AND STOCKHOLDERS' EQUITY

Current Liabilities

Notes payable	$ 200,000
Long-term debt—current payments	50,000
Accounts payable	300,000
Accrued taxes	110,000
Total current liabilities	660,000
Long-Term Debt (less current payments)	300,000
Total Liabilities	960,000

(continues)

Figure 5a. (Continued)

Shareholders' Equity

Common stock, no par value,	
250 shares authorized	
Issued and outstanding	30,000
Retained earnings	86,500
Total stockholders' equity	116,500
Total Liabilities and Stockholders' Equity	$1,076,500

sole proprietorship with one commissioned sales representative. Study the financials for Company B carefully, and then ask yourself the following questions. The answers to these questions are given after the income statement for Company B.

1. Is the company profitable?
2. Is it carrying much debt?
3. Does the cost of sale seem high, low, or about right?
4. Are there operating costs that are missing?
5. Do you see any operating expenses that seem out of line?
6. Would you classify this company as a high-profit organization worthy of your consideration?

Here are the answers to the previous questions on Company B.

1. Yes.
2. No.
3. High.
4. Rent.
5. Question the owner closely on the bad-debt figure. Is it a one-time expense? What has been the history over the past five years? Question travel and entertainment, also. Is any part of the total really a personal expense?
6. Yes.

Once you feel comfortable cruising through the financials, your next step is to look at the company's recent performance record. If possible, go back at least five years. This is important because last year's track record may not be typical. What you need to know is: Has the company been *consistently* profitable? Has the company been growing steadily? Are operating expenses consistent from year to

Figure 5b.   Income statement for Company A.

STATEMENT OF INCOME & RETAINED EARNINGS
YEAR ENDING DECEMBER 31, 19___

SALES	$2,000,000
Cost of sales	1,200,000
Gross profit	800,000
Operating Expenses	
Salaries	250,000
Consulting/contracting	25,000
Payroll taxes	17,000
Lease payments	35,000
Utilities	12,000
Telephone	6,000
Advertising	30,000
Repairs	2,000
Insurance	9,000
Travel & entertainment	41,000
Depreciation	60,000
Auto expense	20,000
Taxes	7,000
Office supplies	14,000
Shipping	19,000
Legal & accounting	3,000
Dues & subscriptions	1,000
Miscellaneous	3,000
Total Operating Expenses	554,000
Other Expenses	
Interest	150,000
Income Before Taxes	$ 96,000

Figure 6a.   Balance sheet for Company B.

BALANCE SHEET
YEAR ENDING DECEMBER 31, 19___

ASSETS

Current Assets	
Cash	$ 3,000
Accounts receivable	9,500
Fixed Assets	
Equipment	9,000
Vehicle	12,500
Less: Accumulated depreciation	(10,000)
Net fixed assets	11,500
Other Assets	
Long-term contract	8,000
Total Assets	$32,000

LIABILITIES AND STOCKHOLDERS' EQUITY

Current Liabilities	
Note payable—vehicle	$ 2,500
Accounts payable	1,000
Total current liabilities	3,500
Long-Term Debt (less current payments)	000
Total liabilities	3,500
Shareholders' Equity	
Retained earnings	7,500
Current earnings	21,000
Total stockholders' equity	28,500
Total Liabilities and Stockholders' Equity	$32,000

Figure 6b.   Income statement for Company B.

STATEMENT OF INCOME & RETAINED EARNINGS
YEAR ENDING DECEMBER 31, 19__

SALES	$250,000
Cost of sales	
Printing	80,000
Commissions	45,000
Gross profit	125,000
Operating expenses	
Bad debt	2,500
Advertising	1,000
Depreciation	4,000
Insurance	1,000
Utilities/maintenance	500
Interest	300
Telephone	1,500
Legal & accounting	500
Office supplies	4,000
Vehicle expense	1,500
Travel & entertainment	8,000
Miscellaneous	1,000
Total Operating Expenses	25,800
Income Before Taxes	99,200
Provision for Income Tax	3,000
Net Income	$ 96,200

---

year? Your odds are dramatically improved if you bet on a proven pattern of steady success.

By now you're quite familiar with financial statements. You also know that they can be as misleading as they are enlightening. Many accountants and business brokers jokingly call the profit and loss statement the pretend and lie statement. To keep the stockholders happy, public corporations want to show as much profit as possible.

Owners of privately held companies try very hard to show as small a profit as possible. They pay through the company every expense they can before the money is taxed, a practice far preferable to paying that same expense out-of-pocket with after-tax dollars.

Obtaining a true picture of the cash thrown off in a small company is sometimes difficult. Business owners try to shelter as much as possible. That's why you'll see company-owned cars, high travel expenses, relatives on the payroll who do little work, and unusually high legal and accounting costs on the P&L. This practice is not necessarily illegal, although some owners push the limits.

Owner Benefit—The Truth About Profitability

The true value of a small business is directly related to its ability to generate profit for the owner. To get an accurate figure that reflects the actual benefit to the owner, you must recast or readjust the company financial statements. In other words, you must extract the direct benefits to the owner that are hidden in the business expenses. We refer to that figure as owner benefit, or seller's discretionary cash. It's the total of all the financial benefits accrued by the owner. Make a note of that term; we'll be referring to it often. Owner benefit is the true measure of a small company's performance. The owner benefit figure is the basis for most business valuation formulas. In order to establish that figure, it's necessary to reconstruct or adjust the income statement (P&L) to reflect the true cash-flow picture.

When you prepare an adjusted profit and loss statement to find the true owner benefit of a company, you'll have constructed a before-and-after income statement. The actual, or the before, statement was constructed for tax purposes. The adjusted P&L, or the after, reflects the actual profit to the owner. You'll probably see some improvement in positive cash flow. Here's how to do it.

Study the following working example to help you understand how to determine true owner benefit. It includes a sample balance sheet and income statement (Figure 7) to work from, a worksheet to use to adjust the P&L to reconstruct the owner benefit, and a sample completed owner benefit worksheet derived from the sample financials, including explanations of all adjustments.

Looking at the adjusted profit and loss worksheet (Figure 8), you'll see four entries at the top: gross sales, cost of sales, other income, and gross profit. Record those figures from the actual income statement. Be careful about the gross sales figure. Make sure that the number does not reflect something other than revenue from the sale

Figure 7a. Balance sheet for Company A.

BALANCE SHEET
YEAR ENDING DECEMBER 31, 19___

ASSETS

Current Assets

Cash	$ 2,000
Accounts receivable	17,500
Inventory	312,000
Due from officers	200,500
Total current assets	532,000

Fquipment

Leasehold improvements	24,500
Auto	45,000
Equipment	250,000
Less: Accumulated depreciation	(150,000)
Net property & equipment	169,500

Other Assets

Real estate	375,000
Total Assets	$1,076,500

LIABILITIES AND STOCKHOLDERS' EQUITY

Current Liabilities

Notes payable	$ 200,000
Long-term debt—current payments	50,000
Accounts payable	300,000
Accrued taxes	110,000
Total current liabilities	660,000
Long-Term Debt (less current payments)	300,000
Total Liabilities	960,000

(continues)

Figure 7a. (Continued)

Shareholders' Equity	
Common stock, no par value, 250 shares authorized	
Issued and outstanding	30,000
Retained earnings	86,500
Total stockholders' equity	116,500
Total Liabilities and Stockholders' Equity	$1,076,500

of the company's products and services, such as income from the sale of assets—real estate, for example. You'll find all of these numbers on the income statement (P&L). Next, you'll see a list under the heading Operating Expenses, with three blank columns directly to the right of each entry. Go through the operating expenses on the income statement line item by line item, and record the actual amount listed in the column titled Actual. Notice that we've left some blank lines for categories not covered on the form.

Now comes the fascinating part—figuring out exactly how much cash benefit has been accrued by the owner. Using the figures from the Actual column, you must determine if the expense is a normal cost of running the business, one that would most likely recur under new ownership. If so, record the same number in the third column, titled Normal Expense.

The middle column, called Nonrecurring/Owner Benefit, is where you record the cash that was of direct benefit to the owner. As you go through the expenses again, line item by line item, you'll have to exercise judgment and caution. The goal is to isolate what could reasonably be called either owner benefit, those expenses that are not necessary business expenses, or expenses that are unusual one-time costs that are not likely to recur in the future. Nonrecurring expenses might include items such as replacing a roof, settling a long-term lawsuit, or automating the entire production facility.

As you review actual costs, you may discover that the operating cost for certain items is less than what you'd consider essential. Let's take advertising costs, for example. If the business you're considering is dependent on advertising, what is the norm for competitors of the same size? Although the current owner may have some good reason for a low figure, you may have to adjust the figure upward to reflect what your actual expenses are likely to be.

Figure 7b. Income statement for Company A.

STATEMENT OF INCOME & RETAINED EARNINGS
YEAR ENDING DECEMBER 31, 19___

SALES	$2,000,000
Cost of sales	1,200,000
Gross profit	800,000
Operating Expenses	
Salaries	250,000
Consulting/contracting	25,000
Payroll taxes	17,000
Lease payments	35,000
Utilities	12,000
Telephone	6,000
Advertising	30,000
Repairs	2,000
Insurance	9,000
Travel & entertainment	41,000
Depreciation	60,000
Auto expense	20,000
Taxes	7,000
Office supplies	14,000
Shipping	19,000
Legal & accounting	3,000
Dues & subscriptions	1,000
Miscellaneous	3,000
Total Operating Expenses	554,000
Other Expenses	
Interest	150,000
Income Before Taxes	$ 96,000

Figure 8a.   Worksheet for adjusted profit and loss statement.

FOR _____ TIME PERIOD _____

Gross sales _____
Cost of sales _____
Other income _____
Gross profit _____

OPERATING EXPENSES:

	Actual	*Nonrecurring/ owner benefit*	*Normal expenses*
Advertising	_____	_____	_____
Bad debts	_____	_____	_____
Bank charges	_____	_____	_____
Car & truck	_____	_____	_____
Commissions	_____	_____	_____
Contributions	_____	_____	_____
Depreciation	_____	_____	_____
Dues/pub.	_____	_____	_____
Employee ben.	_____	_____	_____
Utilities	_____	_____	_____
Insurance	_____	_____	_____
Interest	_____	_____	_____
Legal/prof.	_____	_____	_____
Office supplies	_____	_____	_____
Rent	_____	_____	_____
Repairs/ maint.	_____	_____	_____
Taxes	_____	_____	_____
Travel/entert.	_____	_____	_____
Telephone	_____	_____	_____
Payroll	_____	_____	_____
Payroll taxes	_____	_____	_____
Post/freight	_____	_____	_____
_____	_____	_____	_____

Totals			
Net profit			
Owner benefit			

Another example is rent. Perhaps the owner owns the building and leases it back to his company at an unusually low figure. Unless you can lock in the same numbers with a long-term lease, once again you'll have to adjust the rent figure upward to reflect your situation.

Let's look at some other examples. Suppose the figure in the car and truck category is $15,000. And let's suppose that the business has no need for the vehicle. Obviously, the owner is running a personal expense through the business. When you own the business, you can decide how to use that cash; it's profit and should be recorded as owner benefit in the middle column. On the other hand, if the vehicle is a delivery truck used exclusively for business, the $15,000 figure is a normal operating expense with no owner benefit. You therefore record zero in the Owner Benefit column and $15,000 in the Normal column.

There's another possibility here. Many business owners use their vehicles partly for business and partly for personal use. In this case you must determine the proportion of the operating expense that is personal. Do the same for insurance, licensing, and repairs. Then record that figure in the Owner Benefit column.

Now you can see why you need excellent rapport with the current owner. Without it, it's difficult to get a good sense of what's really owner benefit. Since the owner has a vested interest in showing you how profitable the business has been, you should have little trouble getting him to cooperate, assuming you've done a good job of creating an atmosphere of trust.

Look closely at bad debts. Does the figure line up with what the company has experienced historically? If you find an unusually high figure, perhaps it's because a key customer went belly up. That's a nonrecurring expense. It's very unusual and unlikely to occur again, or so you'd hope. At any rate, it's not a normal operating expense, and the business did generate the cash to cover it. Record it in the middle column as a nonrecurring expense.

Depreciation is a concept that is often misunderstood. Essentially, it's a dollar amount that is set aside to replace assets that wear out. However, most businesses do not actually set the money aside.

Figure 8b. Adjusted profit and loss statement for Company A.

For _____ Company A _____   Time Period _____

Gross sales		$2,000,000
Cost of sales		1,200,000
Other income		
Gross profit		$ 800,000

OPERATING EXPENSES:	Actual	Nonrecurring/ owner benefit	Normal expenses
Advertising	30,000		30,000
Bad debts			
Bank charges			
Car & truck	20,000	20,000	
Commissions			
Contributions			
Depreciation	60,000	60,000	
Dues/pub.	1,000	750	250
Employee ben.			
Utilities	12,000	7,000	5,000
Insurance	9,000	5,000	4,000
Interest	150,000		150,000
Legal/prof.	3,000		3,000
Office supplies	14,000	7,000	7,000
Rent/lease	35,000		35,000
Repairs/maint.	2,000	1,000	1,000
Taxes	7,000	3,000	4,000

Travel/entert.	41,000	20,000	21,000
Telephone	6,000		6,000
Payroll	250,000	150,000	100,000
Payroll taxes	17,000	12,000	5,000
Post/freight	19,000		19,000
Consulting	25,000	25,000	
Misc.	3,000		3,000
Totals	704,000	310,750	393,250
Net profit	96,000	————	————
Owner benefit	406,750	————	————

It only looks that way on the financials. The government is saying, "We realize your equipment will wear out or become obsolete and need to be replaced. Therefore we'll allow you to deduct as an expense a certain amount each year, to take care of replacement costs." The effect is the same as if the allowance were really cash.

Depreciation is a noncash business expense, sometimes called funny money. It's allowed as a legitimate cost of doing business, even though no cash is paid out. Since it's a cash benefit to the owner, record the depreciation figure as owner benefit.

Depreciation is tricky. Here's why. If the fixed assets have been fully depreciated or nearly so and you buy the business as a stock sale, you may have little to depreciate. If the business is an asset sale, rather than a stock sale, you may be able to depreciate the assets on the basis of their current market value. It's a good idea to seek the advice of your accountant here. Although this may indeed be funny money, it can make a big difference in your bottom line.

Under employee benefits, payroll, and taxes, determine what portion can be attributed to owner benefit, and record it. Do the same with each and every item listed as an operating expense. Other items that are commonly considered add-backs to the owner benefit column are pension and profit sharing, personal travel, and disability and health insurance.

Here's an explanation of the owner benefit analysis for Company A.

1. Advertising costs are a normal operating expense. Thirty thousand dollars was spent. There was no benefit to the owner personally.
2. The owner leases his new Jaguar through the company. The automobile is not used for business purposes. It's a perk to the owner and is therefore listed in the owner benefit column.
3. Depreciation is listed as owner benefit. It's one of the benefits of business ownership.
4. Under dues/publications, only $250 was actual business expense. The other $750 was for books and computer software used by the owner's family.
5. Utility costs were $5,000 for the business; $7,000 were costs associated with operating a second business on the premises. Since that business was running at a substantial loss, the owner allocated the $7,000 figure to his highly profitable business in order to get the deduction. That $7,000 is a nonrecurring expense for any new owner.
6. Of the $9,000 insurance figure, $5,000 went for health, life, and disability insurance on the business owner.
7. Under office supplies, half of the amount was for personal purchases.
8. A total of $1,000 of the repair/maintenance account was for personal use.
9. Note the tax in two categories (taxes and payroll taxes) that are owner benefit.
10. Of the $41,000 spent on travel and entertainment, $20,000 was personal.
11. The owner and his spouse paid themselves $150,000 out of the payroll account. The spouse, by the way, spent little time at the business.
12. The $25,000 consulting fee was spent for assistance in developing a five-year marketing plan. Since it's a one-time cost that will not recur as an operating expense, it's listed in the nonrecurring column.

When you're finished, here's what you should have:

1. Under the Actual column, a list of all operating expenses shown on the income statement.
2. Under the column Normal Expenses, a list of all costs that are usual and necessary business expenses. Extract any that ben-

efit the owner or that won't recur, and adjust any that are below what would be considered normal.

3. In the middle column, a list of all expenses that are owner benefit or nonrecurring costs.

The next step is to total each of the three columns. The sum of column one (Actual) always equals the combined sums of columns two (Nonrecurring/Owner Benefit) and three (Normal). If you increase advertising, rent, or repairs because they're too low, be sure to reflect your adjustment in the Owner Benefit column, even if it means a negative number. Otherwise, you won't be able to figure out why the total of column two plus column three doesn't add up to the total of column one.

To find the total owner benefit, add the company's net profit and the total of column two (Nonrecurring or Owner Benefit expenses). The net profit is the gross profit less the actual operating expenses (column one).

To summarize: The net profit added to the nonrecurring or owner benefit expenses equals the total owner benefit. This total is the available cash you have to work with. You can call it profit, owner benefit, disposable cash, or whatever you want. It's the cash thrown off by the business that will go to pay for your debt, salary, and anything else you decide is appropriate. And it's the figure you need to plug into small business valuation formulas in order to determine a selling price for the business.

As you analyze this owner benefit example, you may wonder about the legality of some of the claimed operating costs. However, the issue is not to question the owner's decisions, but rather to get an accurate view of the actual cash flow. The truth is that many business owners take an extremely liberal view of the tax laws.

Remember this: Don't ever take the financials at face value. Financial statements in most small businesses are prepared only at the end of the year to minimize tax liability. Although they should be used as a management tool all year long, all too often they are not.

A company may be far more profitable than the financial statements indicate. The reverse may also be true. Although the example here clearly shows that substantial owner benefit is hidden in the operating costs, you may also find companies that have operating expenses that are far less than those that you would incur. For example, you may find family members working many hours for little or no compensation, or inadequate liability insurance. Remember, when you're doing the owner benefit analysis, if the operating expenses are low or missing, you must plug in the figures that reflect what the actual operating expenses should be.

Financial Management: A Required Skill

If you're new to the world of finance, this chapter may have thrown you. Don't panic. This is not exactly light reading. Go through it again, slowly. Make sure you understand each concept, and refer to the examples often. You'll soon be able to evaluate the health of any company you may be considering.

You'll also develop financial management skills that will be very useful as you manage your newly acquired company. You'll be able to deal easily with questions like: Are my operating expenses in line? Is my pricing okay? Can I afford to hire that new employee? Is now the time to invest in that new equipment? You will understand the language of business.

11

It's All in the Numbers

How to Calculate the Sales Price

Now that you have a working knowledge of financial statements and the real story they tell, you're ready to establish the market value of your target company in order to arrive at a fair sales price. Remember, of course, that a fair price in your mind is almost certain to be different from a fair price in the mind of the seller. The question we must deal with now, however, is: How do you establish the true market value of your company?

You may think that valuing a company is a precise science. After all, establishing the book value or net worth is pretty straightforward once you understand the financials. But book value is only one of many factors determining market value. Many tangible and intangible factors must be considered in order to reach a reasonable sales price on a business.

Thick books have been written on business valuation. It can be an incredibly complex topic. Your purpose here is not to become an investment banker or a business appraisal expert. Rather, it's to establish a ballpark market price from which you and the seller can negotiate a final selling price that both parties can live with. And remember this: A well-prepared business valuation supported by documentation from the company's financial statements is your best assurance of negotiating a final price that the seller and his advisers will take seriously.

The selling price for a small business is primarily related to the company's ability to generate consistent profits. Why? Because that's why most people buy a business in the first place. There may be other reasons to own a business, but its worth in the marketplace is directly tied to its ability to generate cash.

The Rule of Two-Thirds

No matter what the final figure, there are three fundamental factors to consider. All three are related to cash flow. First and foremost, the company must have the capability of servicing from cash flow the debt you've taken on to acquire the business. Very few small businesses sell for all cash for the same reason that most real estate doesn't. Buyers usually carry debt of between one-half to two-thirds of the purchase price. Terms vary; however, from three to seven years financed at or around the going interest rate is common.

Any business that you are considering that cannot service the debt is a bad investment, no matter how attractive it may be in other respects. Either lower the purchase price substantially or walk away. How far you're willing to bend to own the business is, of course, your decision. But here's a rule of thumb to help with your decision. Called the Rule of Two-Thirds, it states: "If the business will not support a debt service of two-thirds of the purchase price, pass or lower the purchase price."

This rule of thumb assumes a down payment of one-third. Even if you're putting down more, the business still should be generating enough profit to cover two-thirds of the sales price; otherwise you're paying too much. Certainly there are exceptions to this rule, but it's valid in most cases.

By the way, you'll need a book of interest amortization schedules. It's a required tool to evaluate any situation you may be considering. With it, you'll be able to compute any number of possible debt scenarios.

In addition to servicing debt, your prospective company must give you a reasonable return on your down payment. After all, if you placed that amount in some other investment vehicle, you'd expect a reasonable return, wouldn't you?

And third, even though you're excited about becoming a captain of industry, you still must buy the groceries, pay the mortgage, and clothe the kids. How much you need to live on is, of course, a personal matter. However, a good rule of thumb is to plug in a figure for a living wage approximately equal to what you'd have to pay a manager to run the company.

A fair return on the down payment, salary and benefits, and debt service capability are the three factors that you must consider when computing a reasonable purchase price. Of course, the tangible value of fixed assets and inventory will be factored in, but it's the intangible value of the business that makes the business what it is. It's also what makes it difficult to price. If the cash flow will cover what we call "the basic three," you've got an attractive company to consider.

We're not interested in precision here. We're interested in getting to a point where we know the ballpark figure is realistic. Since the price you propose to the seller will be the subject of much negotiation, the final selling price will most likely be different, perhaps substantially different. So let's talk about how to peg that ballpark figure.

Valuing Small Private Companies

There are many reasons for valuing a business. Estate planning, preparation for reorganization, measurement of capital gains or losses, and verification of worth for lenders or investors are only a few. Your purpose is to value the business to establish the current market price. Therefore you'll consider some factors unimportant and others quite critical. For example, lenders may be very concerned about the value of fixed assets. You may consider them relatively unimportant.

Second, the concern here is with small, privately held companies. Publicly held corporations are often valued differently.

Finally, no matter what formula you use to value the company, in the mind of the seller it will be the wrong one. He'll counter with his own formula, designed to justify his higher sales price. Therefore, you must value the company using several different valuation methods in order to document your proposed figure.

Remember, no matter what valuation method is employed, arriving at an accurate market value except for liquidation sales always relies heavily on an accurate analysis of the company's cash flow. Unfortunately, some companies have no value other than the auction value of their fixed assets. But let's assume you're dealing with a going concern, a healthy and profitable company.

As mentioned earlier, there are many, many ways to value a business. You may have heard of valuation methods called workouts and formulas for determining value on the basis of future profits adjusted for inflation. There are many others that are used by investment bankers. Happily, you can ignore them. The formulas used to value small businesses are fewer and simpler. And they work.

If you use the ones outlined here, you'll have the essentials to value just about any small company that interests you.

Work closely with your accountant, however. Since every business is unique, it's important to check any valuation with an accountant before presenting it to a business owner.

Asset Valuation

The first formula is called the asset valuation. Use this formula when the company is asset-intensive. Although another formula may result in a lower figure, you can be sure that the owner's financial advisor will use a valuation formula that takes the value of assets into account.

For an asset valuation, first you must have the value of the company's fixed assets and furniture, fixtures, and equipment. Generally, the value can be looked at in four ways. One is replacement value, which is what it would cost to replace the assets and equipment in today's dollars. That's fine for insurance purposes, but not for valuations. You're not going to replace it. You're going to use it the way it is.

Scrap value or liquidation value is also not appropriate. You don't plan to liquidate anytime soon (you hope). Depreciated value can be taken directly off the balance sheet. But that's an accounting figure for tax purposes. Frequently it bears no relationship whatsoever to the real worth of the assets.

What you need to know is the market value of the fixed assets and equipment. Market value is the price you would pay if you were to buy each asset or piece of equipment on the open market at a price experts in the industry would agree is reasonable.

If the business has a great deal of equipment and fixed assets, it's wise to have an appraisal done. Professional appraisers are available in every region and in every industry. If the asset base is relatively small, or if you're familiar with the industry, you may be able to determine the value by yourself. The owner probably has a very good idea of the actual worth of the equipment and in many cases can be invaluable in helping you arrive at a market value. However, remember it's to his advantage to inflate the worth. Another potential source of help, once again, is your accountant.

To compute an asset valuation, add the market value of fixed assets and equipment to the value of leasehold improvements. Leasehold improvements are additions, modifications, upgrades, renovations, or other changes to the physical property that would be considered part of the property should you sell the property or not renew a lease. You can't take such improvements with you since they are legally considered a permanent addition to the real estate. You'll find the leasehold improvements, if there are any, listed in the financials. Next add the wholesale value of inventory. (Add the value of raw materials, work-in-progress, and finished goods or products to get the total value of inventory. Raw materials are the part of the inventory used to manufacture or fabricate the company's products; work-in-progress means exactly what it says—goods in various stages moving toward becoming a finished product.)

To this total, add the owner's discretionary cash as calculated in your adjusted income statement. The total of all these is the sale price. Once more: The asset valuation is the total of the fair market value of fixed assets and equipment, leasehold improvements, inventory, and one year's owner benefit, or owner's discretionary cash. Essentially, this method states that the business value is equal to the hard assets plus goodwill.

Goodwill, for our purposes, is profit or owner benefit for one year. The term is used to describe the intangible value or soft value of a business. Therefore, it is highly subjective. It is the value of those things on which it is difficult to place a value. Typical items that could be considered goodwill are reputation, loyal and skilled employees, proprietary processes, patents, quality of customer base, and profit consistency.

The asset valuation formula can be stated as an equation:

$$FMV/FA + LHI + OB + I = MV$$

where:

> FMV/FA is the fair market value of the fixed assets, including all the furniture, fixtures, and equipment that would be sold as part of the business.
> LHI is the leasehold improvements.
> OB is the owner benefit, or the seller's discretionary cash flow for a one-year period.
> I is the inventory.
> MV is the market value of the business.

If you were valuing Company A in Chapter 10, using the sample balance sheet, the sample income statement, and the sample adjusted profit and loss statement (see Figures 5a, 5b, and 8b), you would extract the appropriate figures from the sample balance sheet and the adjusted profit and loss statement. Remember the adjusted P&L was constructed using the sample income statement. Here's how it would look:

$$FMV/FA = \$169,500$$
$$LHI = \$\ 24,500$$
$$OB = \$406,750$$
$$I = \$312,000$$

Therefore: $FMV/FA + LHI + OB + I = MV$
($169,500 + $24,500 + $406,750 + $312,000 = $912,750)

The market value of the business according to the asset valuation is $912,750.

Notice that we used the depreciated value of the furniture, fixtures, and equipment taken directly from the balance sheet. In reality, the actual market value may be somewhat more or less. Note that the real estate recorded on the balance sheet was not included. In cases where the real estate is part of the sale, its market value is added. In this case, as in all these formulas, we are valuing the business alone.

Remember: Use this formula when the business is asset-intensive. Although bank financing is the exception in small-business acquisitions by individuals, if you do use bank financing the asset valuation will be required by the lending officer to determine a figure against which the note can be secured.

Capitalization of Income Valuation

The second valuation method is called the capitalization of income formula. Unlike the asset formula, this method places no value on the equipment and other fixed assets. It's assumed that they have no value other than the ability to produce income for the company. Service companies, which are often not asset-intensive, are often valued using this method.

This valuation method acknowledges the business's intangible value, or goodwill. After all, a business is much more than assets and the profit it produces. The question is, how much more? Again, since goodwill is so subjective, it's difficult to place a number on its value. But don't despair. There is a way to assign a value to the intangible side of the business, and by adding it to what will be your available cash flow, you can peg a sales price. Here's how.

The first requirement is to reduce the intangible value of a business to a list of factors that most commonly affect its value.

Twelve factors are listed in the Capitalization of Income Rate Multiplier Factors. The trick is to place an appropriate value on each. Rate each factor on a scale of zero to five, with five being the highest, most positive score.

Capitalization of Income Rate Multiplier Factors
1. *The owner's reason for selling.* The more urgent the reason, the lower the score.
2. *Length of time the company has been in business.* Obviously, the longer, the better.
3. *Length of time the current owner has owned the business.* Again, longevity gets a high score.
4. *Degree of risk.* High-risk businesses, such as restaurants or retail stores, get low marks.
5. *Profitability.* Does the company show acceptable and consistent profit margins for the last five years? (Remember, profit in a small business is owner benefit. Reported net profit is often intentionally nonexistent for tax purposes.)
6. *Business location.* Is the business in the right area of the country and the right part of town? Do employees and customers find the location attractive? Is there an adequate employee pool?
7. *Growth history.* Have gross revenues shown acceptable increases over the last five years?
8. *Competition.* Are there a few or many competing companies? Does the company have a competitive advantage?
9. *Entry barriers.* How easy is it for competitors to enter the market?
10. *Future potential for the industry.* Is it growing, stable, or declining?
11. *Customer base.* What is the percentage of repeat business? Is the customer list diverse? Growing? What volume of business comes from customer referrals?
12. *Technology.* Does the company have trained personnel, state-of-the-art equipment, and high quality standards?

Let's look at a couple of these factors in more detail.

• *Length of time the company has been in business.* If the current owner began the business a year ago or less, it has the same risk as a start-up. Give it a zero. To receive a five, the business should have at least a ten-year history. Any business without a three-year track record should receive low scores; it hasn't been around long enough to prove itself.

• *Growth history.* Have revenues shown acceptable growth over the last five years? This is very important. It's often been said that unless a business is growing, it's dying. Even if your prospective company has been profitable, lack of growth could signal problems, such as product obsolescence, market saturation, fierce competition, or uncontrolled increases in operating expenses.

Look for annual growth rates of 10–30 percent. Assign a 2.5 to a 15 percent growth rate and maybe a 4.0 to a 30 percent rate. In very small companies that are just starting out, it's not unusual to see growth rates of 300, 400, or even 500 percent. However, that's usually short-lived. Twenty to 30 percent is very healthy and allows the business owner to stay in control.

• *Customer base.* What is the percentage of repeat business? How diverse are the customers? Is their number growing? How much growth is coming from customer referrals? One of the most important assets of a business is its customer list. A business without a stable of loyal customers who generate repeat revenue over the long haul isn't worth much. Obviously, a company that is well known and highly regarded by a large customer base will receive a high score. One without any repeat business or name recognition earns a low score.

• *Future potential for the industry.* Is it growing, stable, or declining? No matter how motivated you may be, it's difficult to grow your business if the market is dead or dying. If the market is stable, you may have to increase business by stealing it from competitors. In a growth market, there may be enough business for everyone. So assign a zero, or at best a one, to a declining market. A high growth market might receive a four or five.

Go through the rest of the factors on the list, and assign a value to each. By the way, it should be clear that this exercise is impossible unless you've done your homework and know both the industry and the company extremely well.

Now, total the figures and divide by twelve. The resulting figure is the multiplier that plugs into the cap rate formula. Next, take the owner benefit figure (seller's discretionary cash) and multiply it by 75 percent. The result is what is called buyer's discretionary cash, or what you will have after allocating 25 percent of the cash thrown off by the business to service debt. (Most business brokers use this 25 percent debt service figure because experience has shown that the majority of deals close with about one-third down and two-thirds of the purchase price financed.) To arrive at the selling price, the final step is to multiply the buyer's discretionary cash by the cap rate multiplier.

For the sake of example, let's assign a cap rate of 3 to Company A. Again, using the figures from the sample company in Chapter 10, the market value of the business would be computed as follows:

$$Cap\ Rate \times BDC = MV$$

where:

> *Cap rate* is the capitalization rate, which is the average of the twelve factors listed earlier.
> *BDC* is the buyer's discretionary cash, equal to 75 percent of the seller's discretionary cash (owner benefit).
> *MV* is the market value of the business.

If you were using the same financial data as you used when valuing the business using the asset formula, the number would look like this:

$$Cap\ Rate = 3$$
$$BDC = 75\%$$
$$SDC = 75\% \times 406,750 = 305,062.50$$
$$(3 \times 305,062.50) = Market\ Value\ of\ \$915,187.50$$

Seller's Discretionary Cash or Owner Benefit Valuation

Here's another formula that focuses on the seller's discretionary cash flow, or owner benefit. Used to value businesses whose primary value comes from an ability to generate cash flow and profit, it's called the Seller's Discretionary Cash Formula. Multiply the owner's discretionary cash times debt service. Remember, the standard figure is 25 percent. Divide that number by 1.1, which is a standard for return on investment. The formula assumes that if you invested that amount of money in a relatively safe investment, you could earn a 10 percent return. The resulting figure is then divided by 0.3, which gives you the sales price. (The 0.3 figure derives from the assumption that most buyers will allow about a third of the discretionary cash for their living wage.)

But you don't have to go through each step to make this formula work. Simply multiply the seller's discretionary cash by a composite factor of 2.2727, and presto—you have the sales price.

The equation is this simple:

$$SDC \times 2.2727 = MV$$

where:

> *SDC* is the seller's discretionary cash, or owner benefit.
> 2.2727 is the composite multiplier to adjust for return on investment, living wage, and debt service.
> *MV* is the market value of the business.

Once again, plugging in the number for Company A, here's the market value or sales price:

$$SDC = \$406,750$$
$$\$406,750 \times 2.2727 = \$924,420$$

Industry Multipliers

The fourth formula is actually a long list of formulas that apply to specific industries. They're called industry multipliers. And many people swear by them. Many other people, particularly buyers, don't like them because they focus on gross sales, rather than net profit or owner benefit, and, as you know by now, it's not the top line that counts. It's the bottom line. The following rule-of-thumb valuation formulas should be used with caution. Although remarkably accurate in some situations, they tend to take an overly simplistic view of business worth. The actual value of a specific business may be very different. Nevertheless, these formulas are useful for nailing down a rough selling price in some cases. Here's a list of some common ones:

Travel agencies:	.05 to .1 × Annual Gross Sales
Advertising agencies:	.75 × Annual Gross Sales
Collection agencies:	.15 to .2 × Annual Collections + Equipment
Employment agencies:	.75 × Annual Gross Sales
Insurance agencies:	1 to 2 × Annual Renewal Commissions
Real estate agencies:	.2 to .3 × Annual Gross Commissions

Rental agencies:	.2 × Annual Net Profit + Inventory
Retail businesses:	.75 to 1.5 × Annual Net Profit + Inventory + Equipment
Sales businesses:	1 × Annual Net Profit
Fast food (nonfranchise):	.5 to .7 × Monthly Gross Sales + Inventory
Restaurants:	.3 to .5 × Annual Gross Sales, or .4 × Monthly Gross Sales + Inventory
Office supply distributors:	.5 × Monthly Gross Sales + Inventory
Newspapers:	75 to 1.5 × Annual Gross Sales
Printers:	.4 to .5 × Annual Net Profit + Inventory + Equipment
Food distributors:	1 to 1.5 × Annual Net Profit + Inventory + Equipment
Building supply retailers:	.25 to .75 Annual Net Profit + Inventory + Equipment
Job shops:	.5 × Annual Gross Sales + Inventory
Manufacturing:	1.5 to 2.5 × Annual Net Profit + Inventory .75 × Annual Net Profit + Equipment + Inventory (including work in progress)
Farm/heavy equipment dealers:	.5 × Annual Net Profit + Inventory + Equipment
Professional practices:	1 to 5 × Annual Net Profit
Boat/camper dealers:	1 × Annual Net Profit + Inventory + Equipment

After you've become comfortable with the valuation formulas, try them out on a prospective company. You'll be surprised how easy it is once you've gone through it a couple of times. Use all the formulas. As you gain experience, you'll see that one formula seems to be more appropriate than the others for the type of company you're valuating.

You'll also find that, more often than not, you'll arrive at about the same figure using several of the formulas, although sometimes one may give you a figure wildly apart from the others. Note the closeness of the three selling prices arrived at in the formulas used to value Company A. If two or more formulas get you to roughly the same selling price, it's a good indicator that your valuation process is on target.

It's a good idea to do a valuation for each of the last three years.

After all, last year's figures may be an anomaly. In an unstable or developing market, revenue swings may be dramatic. In some cases, you may want to go back further than three years. Although the seller won't be wild about it, it's not uncommon to average the last three years to arrive at the numbers used in a valuation formula.

Once you're comfortable that you know what you're doing, you'll quickly come to see that arriving at a ballpark selling price isn't mysterious at all. There's a logical process that gives you solid data to justify to the seller your fair and reasonable price.

12

Win-Win Negotiation

The Secrets of Effective Deal Making

Doing a deal is both art and science. Professionals who negotiate for a living will tell you that preparation and documentation are the key success factors. They'll also tell you that closing good deals consistently requires the ability to focus on the needs of both parties. Arriving at a point where both sides leave the table feeling that a fair and equitable arrangement has been struck doesn't just happen by magic. It's the result of executing a well-planned strategy.

Before we move on to a discussion of how to design and implement a negotiation strategy, it's important that you understand what negotiating is and what it isn't. It isn't a contest where someone wins and someone loses. Unfortunately, most of what we've learned about how to negotiate assumes that, with the help of some fancy techniques, it's possible to outmaneuver the competition and win the game, while the loser licks his wounds and wonders what happened.

Buying a business is not an athletic contest. It's actually more like a marriage. Do you look at your marriage and ask, "Who's winning?" Of course not! It's a relationship in which both parties work together to satisfy not only their own needs but the needs of their partner as well.

When you think about it, buying a business is similar in some ways. The seller has a desire to get out of a business. You have a desire to get into a business. The seller doesn't have to sell. You don't have to buy. Neither side can force the other to do what he or she doesn't want to do.

Therefore, the only thing that makes sense is to figure out a way for both buyer and seller to come out winners. Rather than win-lose, it's win-win. Win-win negotiation, although simple in concept, requires a change in your basic assumptions. As long as you think of negotiations as a contest to be won, you'll find the results less than satisfying. When you think of it as a process by which to solve a problem to the satisfaction of buyer and seller, creative solutions begin to form.

Why? Because both parties now have the same goal—to achieve a sale where the buyer can afford to buy a profitable company and the seller is able to cash out in a way that makes sense.

However, before you get down to brass tacks, you must develop a relationship of trust and understanding, a relationship in which both parties genuinely like one another. It's astounding how few businesspeople understand how significant this is. People who don't like you will find a reason not to do business with you. And if they don't trust you, forget it.

Think about the really successful business people you know. Chances are they are very likeable people. Their word is their bond, and they can be trusted implicitly. Great leaders, salespeople, managers, and teachers can get people to move when others can't budge them. Their people skills are more important than any technical know-how.

Obviously, it takes time to create the right kind of relationship. You didn't ask your spouse to marry you on the first date, did you? The more meetings you have with the seller before beginning serious negotiations, the better. Go to lunch. If possible, visit customers with the seller. Remember, you don't have to tell the customer you're considering buying the business. Visit vendors. Play golf or tennis. Do whatever you can to allow the relationship to develop. You'll accomplish two goals. One, you'll form a fruitful relationship. Two, you'll learn a good deal about the company.

Proposing Your Deal

Okay, you've done your homework. You understand the industry, the market, the company. Certainly, the completion of your analysis and valuation is an important step in deciding whether to buy a business. But remember that the seller must make an equally important decision—whether or not to sell. That decision will be heavily influenced by how well you present your case.

If you've successfully developed a relationship with the seller, it's time to sit down and cut a deal. It's common practice in today's business world to present major business changes in the form of a written proposal. For the seller, this change is about as major as you can get. Remember, the owner of the business that you'd like to buy will sell only if it's in his or her best interest. Therefore, you must present a strong case that clearly documents the personal benefits to the owner of selling the business to you.

No matter how good you may be in presenting your case in person, back it up with a written proposal. There are several reasons. First of all, the owner won't remember most of what you said. Later, when he's seriously contemplating your offer, the probability is high that your most compelling arguments will be long forgotten. Second, since most owners will seek advice from both professional and personal sources, a written proposal is a strong sales aid to help convince well-meaning but skeptical advisers that the deal is a good one. Finally, the proposal presents you as an exceptional business professional. Not one in a hundred will go to the trouble of creating a powerful business proposal like yours. Just think about how impressed you'd be if you were the seller.

The Letter of Intent

Begin by presenting a letter of intent. A letter of intent is not a formal offer to purchase the business. Rather, it's a proposal that outlines your thinking regarding the key issues of the purchase. Because this document can become legally binding, it should be constructed with extreme care. Every section should be cleared with your accountant and the final document approved by your attorney. It's difficult to regain things you didn't intend to give away in the first place.

What's in a letter of intent? Several things. Of greatest interest to the seller will be the financial arrangement you're proposing. State the proposed purchase price and the down payment. Remember that your initial position on a selling price should be somewhat less than the top price you'd eventually agree to pay. For that reason, leave out of your proposal any discussion of the valuation formulas used.

State the amount of any promissory note and the duration and interest rate for that note. If you're also proposing a balloon payment, supply the details. If you're offering a percentage of future revenue or profits as part of your payment, how will the process work? (This arrangement, called a workout, is a very popular way to resolve a problem when the seller and buyer can't agree on the selling price. Essentially, you offer to pay a base price for the company and add an additional bonus based on the future performance of the company, usually a small percentage of the revenue over a certain amount for a period of three to five years. In some cases, there's a cap on the high end. In instances where the seller will stay on as an employee, the performance bonus is often tied to profitability, rather than to revenue.)

Contingencies of the Sale

In addition to the sales price and the payment terms, there are a host of other issues, commonly referred to as contingencies of the sale, that are important to resolve if the deal is going to fly. We suggest that you not specify every issue in the letter of intent. You'll need room to negotiate. In your letter of intent, you should indicate that the sale is predicated upon the satisfactory resolution of particular contingencies, which you then list. The specifics of resolving these contingencies will be the subject of future negotiations.

For example, rather than stating that a consulting fee of $35,000 per year shall be paid to the seller for a period of four years, simply say that a mutually agreeable consulting agreement between buyer and seller shall be reached. You'll decide how to fill in the blanks during the give-and-take of negotiating.

What contingencies should be listed? Obviously, each situation creates its own. However, here are some common ones. If the seller is to stay on as a full-time employee, what's your arrangement with her? If the seller is leaving, you'll need a solid noncompete agreement. Other contingencies may include the assignment of the lease, the allocation of the purchase price, a satisfactory review of the company's books and records, an examination of insurance policies, agreements with key employees to stay on, evidence that key customers won't defect, assurances by the seller that he's responsible for liability claims up to the sale date, and agreement on the length and terms of any training period. The list can get much, much longer.

Purchase Price and Terms

Of course, the most significant issue you must address in your letter of intent is the proposed purchase price. Although you can be quite general about the contingencies of the sale, the seller will expect you to be specific about the price. So state the proposed sale price, the down payment, the size and length of the note, and the interest rate.

To do this, first decide on the absolute top price that you'll pay and the combination of terms and price. If the price ends up exceeding that figure, resolve to walk away. Without the purchase price nailed down, you have no negotiating road map.

Most professional negotiators feel that it's not wise to start at a figure that is ridiculously low. First of all, a seller has a pretty good idea of the company's worth. It's highly unlikely that you'll be able to steal the company. Second, your credibility will be shot, along with the relationship, if your proposal is insultingly unrealistic.

Business negotiators have found that a proposed sale price about 25 percent below and an interest rate 50 percent below what you want is acceptable but gives you room to maneuver. Ask that the length of any note run twice as long as you are actually willing to settle for. Propose a down payment of half what you would really agree to. In your letter of intent, propose a small binder if the offer is accepted to ensure that the business is not sold to someone else and to demonstrate that you're a serious buyer.

Once you've decided on the details of your initial offer and have created a draft of your letter of intent, give copies to your accountant and your lawyer for their input. Make any necessary revisions, and prepare the final document. Be sure to proofread it carefully. It's one of the most important documents you'll ever prepare. Later, if the deal goes through, your lawyer will prepare a formal Purchase and Sales Agreement, the legal document that transfers ownership. Although you should have the Purchase and Sales Agreement prepared by your attorney, the initial offer to purchase, typically in the form of a letter of intent, should be designed and written by you. Because writing the initial proposal to purchase the business will require you to think through the details, you'll be well prepared to make a convincing oral presentation of your proposal. After writing the final draft of your proposal, edit it thoroughly. Prepare the final document on quality paper, with no errors. After completing this exercise, you'll find that presenting your proposal is easy.

The following are two examples of a letter of intent. Read them carefully, and use them as a starting point for developing your own document.

Designing the Negotiation Strategy

You're still not ready to deliver your offer. Negotiating the sale of a business is complex. You'll have to think carefully about whether you have the ability to do most of the actual negotiating yourself. There are some real pluses to doing it personally, but the chance of a serious error is very real and very expensive. This is one of the most critical decisions you'll make. If you have a good relationship with the seller

(Text continues on p. 162.)

Figure 9.   Sample letters of intent.

Example 1

Anne Beck
President
Prescott Systems, Inc.
444 Harding Road
Allentown, PA 18101

April 27, 1993

Dear Anne,

I appreciate the time and energy you've expended to supply the information I've requested over the last few weeks. It's been very helpful in making a solid business decision about the possible purchase of your business. I've constructed a purchase proposal that I feel meets both our needs and at the same time reflects the market value of your business. The purchase price, terms, and conditions are described below.

PURCHASE PRICE:	Base Price	$100,000
	Performance Bonus	$50,000

The Performance Bonus will become part of the total purchase price when and if Prescott Systems' profit before taxes and before provision for buyer's compensation and fringe benefits equals or exceeds 7 percent of net sales for three years from Date of Purchase. Otherwise, the total purchase price shall be $100,000.

PAYMENT TERMS: $50,000 at closing. The remainder of the base price ($50,000) will be repaid in the form of a note, taken back by the seller. The note payments shall be paid quarterly for a term of four years. The first payment shall be ninety days after closing. The interest rate shall be 10 percent based on a four-year amortization schedule, with no prepayment penalties.

If the Performance Bonus is payable, a second note shall be written on January 1, 1995, for $50,000. Interest and terms of payment shall be the same as the first note.

CONDITIONS: The purchase of the business is subject to the following:

1. Buyer shall purchase the assets of the Company and form a New Corporation bearing the same Company name.

2. Buyer shall pledge the assets of the New Corporation as collateral for the note or notes.
3. Buyer and Seller shall develop a mutually agreeable Employment Contract between the Seller and the New Corporation.
4. A Covenant Not to Compete, satisfactory to Buyer, shall be drafted.
5. The existing Lease shall be assigned to the New Corporation with essentially the same terms and conditions.
6. The existing Line of Credit with Consolidated Banking Corp. shall be transferred to the New Corporation under terms satisfactory to the Buyer.
7. Buyer and Seller shall develop a mutually satisfactory Profit-sharing Plan.
8. Upon acceptance of this offer, Seller agrees to allow Buyer and his agents to communicate with customers, employees, and vendors.
9. This offer is subject to recision if the Buyer or his agents are not satisfied with this Offer Agreement, the Purchase and Sales Agreement, the company books and records, or any information from any other source which could change Buyer's assessment of the worth or desirability of the business.
10. Life Insurance shall be secured by the New Corporation on the Buyer's life with the Seller as the only beneficiary. The amount shall equal or exceed the amount due under the terms of the Purchase and Sales Agreement.

Upon acceptance of this offer, Buyer shall pay a $10,000 good faith deposit to a law firm designated by the Seller. Said deposit shall be held in escrow and shall be returned to Buyer if this agreement is not executed within ten days.

If this offer is accepted, the Buyer shall apply the total amount held in escrow as partial payment of the down payment. The date of closing shall be no later than sixty days from the date of this offer.

Sincerely,

J. S. Welch

ACCEPTANCE: Your signature below indicates your agreement to the above.

| Signature | Date |

(continues)

Figure 9.   (Continued)

Example 2

Mr. Ronan Donohoe
President
Harlan WoodProducts
1200 Harbor Cove
Key West, FL 32456

June 11, 1993

Dear Ronan,

I'm certainly impressed with what you've accomplished at Harlan WoodProducts. After having the opportunity to study your company and the market, I share your excitement about the potential.

I would like to buy Harlan WoodProducts and have you continue as President. My role would be Chairman of the Board and Chief Executive Officer. My plan would be to allow you to run all of the day-to-day operations of the Company.

In trying to structure a win-win deal, I've struggled with the problem of your desire to receive a selling price that reflects the potential rather than the actual value based strictly on past performance. Also, since the Company needs additional working capital, I've tried to structure my offer in a way that will allow us to have the money we'll need to meet our growth projections. I believe that the purchase structure described here accomplishes that.

With a combination of cash, debt, salary, bonuses, and royalties, the purchase structure would provide a guaranteed minimum of $750,000 and anticipated payments in excess of $1.5 million over ten years. Since these anticipated payments are based on sales of only 10,000 units, there is considerable upside potential in the package.

The terms are the following:

1. *$200,000 Cash.* I would pay this amount in cash at closing for a portion of your stock.
2. *$150,000 Cash.* I would invest this amount directly in the Company to expand the equity base.
3. *$200,000 Note.* The Company would buy the remainder of your Stock and issue you a Note in the amount of $200,000 paying you

interest only, quarterly at 10 percent for five years, and then 10 percent interest plus principal in quarterly payments over the next five years. The Note could be prepaid by the Company with no prepayment penalty and would be subordinated to other short and long-term debt. I would guarantee the Note with the Harlan WoodProducts Stock that I've purchased.

4. *Five-Year Employment Agreement.* The Company would enter into a Five-Year Employment Agreement with you. The intention would be for you to serve as President for the duration of the Agreement. Your starting salary would be $40,000 per year and escalate by $5,000 per year and would include a President's bonus equal to 10 percent of pretax profits and the use of a company vehicle. The bonus would be paid annually. You would receive the salary as long as you are employed by the Company. If you left, you would receive a minimum of $25,000 per year as a consultant. The bonus and Company vehicle would be provided as long as you held the position of President. We would negotiate a new compensation package in 1994. You would agree not to compete with the Company through the year 1994 or for two years after leaving the Company.

5. *Royalty Payments.* The Company would agree to pay you Royalties through 1999 on current and new products. The Royalty would be 5 percent of Gross Profit over $200,000 per year. A minimum Royalty of $5,000 would be paid each year starting in 1994. The Royalty would be paid quarterly based on interim financial reports and would be adjusted annually based on the final yearly financial statements. You would agree to assign to the Company all inventions and patents through 1994 or for two years after leaving the Company.

6. *Building Lease and Option.* The Company would enter into a Five-Year Lease for the land and building at an initial annual rent equal to the current rent paid by the Company. The rent would escalate by 5 percent per year. The Company would have an option through 1994 to purchase the land and building for $400,000.

While there are a number of details to be worked out, the purchase structure is straightforward. I would be purchasing your stock, and the Company would continue as the same entity. Employees would feel secure since you would still be President, additional capital would go into the Company to help it grow, and an employee profit-sharing plan would be put in place.

If you are in agreement, I would suggest that the next step should be to begin drawing up the legal documents while you and I reach agreement

(continues)

Figure 9.   (Continued)

on five-year projections and complete our due diligence. I will place a good faith deposit of $10,000 in escrow with my attorney.

Our agreement on the terms of this letter in no way obligates either one of us to complete the purchase and sale of the Company Stock. It is understood that such obligation will be binding only upon the execution of final legal documents satisfactory to both of us. If we are unable to reach final agreement, the escrow deposit would, of course, be returned to me.

If you are in agreement with the terms of this letter, please so signify by signing below.

Sincerely,

Max Holly

_____
                         Signature   Date

and you're both willing to put a deal together, the two of you will do a better job at striking a deal than any outsider could. On the other hand, if you don't have a working knowledge of law and taxes, it's wise to have your lawyer handy. Whatever you do, make it clear that all decisions are subject to the approval of your accountant and your lawyer.

If you do decide to go ahead and do your own negotiating, there's homework to do first. Sit down and prepare a list of every conceivable issue that could be raised by you or by the seller. Ask your advisers what you've left out. Then write down your position on each issue and your justification for that position. Although it may be difficult, try to base your arguments on logic, rather than emotion.

Now place yourself in the seller's position and complete the same exercise. This time, be certain to include the emotional arguments as well as the logical ones: It's a sure thing that you'll have to deal with them, too. If this seems like a lot of work, you're right. But remember what's riding on it. Business-acquisition experts routinely go through this exercise. You'll find that the payoff is well worth the effort.

If you've already learned a good deal about the seller, you'll know how he thinks and how he makes decisions, and you'll have some idea of where he'll give and where he won't. That alone will make this entire exercise much easier.

Preparation is the key to concluding a deal satisfactorily. Think through every aspect of the deal. Draw up a list of the benefits that the seller will gain when he sells the business. Include in this list not only the obvious monetary pluses but also the less obvious psychological rewards. By now you should know the seller well enough to know what's really important to him. Press all the hot buttons. If the seller is planning on retiring, list the benefits of selling to you in terms of leisure time, increased quality of life, and opportunity to enjoy favorite hobbies. Perhaps the seller is burned out. Stress the chance to recharge, reinvest, or prepare for a new career. Get all the benefits you can possibly dream up on paper. Use them as an important part of your presentation. Remember: The decision will be made with the heart, as well as the head.

Practice First

It's almost time to go head-to-head with the seller. But there's still one important piece of business to attend to. You must rehearse. The best way to do that is through role playing. Get your spouse or a friend to work with you by playing the role of the seller.

Write out an outline of what you think will happen. Describe in detail the role that you want your friend to take, and then go to it. Practice it again and again. If at all possible, videotape the role play. Chances are excellent that when you view the video, you'll cringe in disbelief: "Was I really that awful?" Yes, you probably were. But you'll learn a great deal from this experience. After the fourth or fifth role play, you'll see dramatic improvement. And think what that will mean when you go "live."

The Moment of Truth: Presenting the Offer

Now it's time for the real thing. Never mail your offer; always deliver it in person. Schedule a meeting where you won't be interrupted. Sit down and explain your proposal in detail to the seller. There are three reasons for this. One, it gives you an opportunity to gauge his reaction to key issues. Two, if you have the opportunity to present your proposal in person, you can prevent misunderstandings concerning the provisions of the proposed sale before they occur. And three, you'll have an opportunity to advance your proposal by documenting with logical arguments why the deal is reasonable and fair.

Don't expect to reach a final agreement at the first meeting. In fact, don't try to negotiate. Indicate that you understand that the seller needs time to digest your proposal. Make certain that each issue is understood, and then agree on a date for your next meeting. That's it for now. Don't push. The last thing the seller wants is to feel pressured. He has a lot to think about, and he needs input from others before he can respond.

Meeting number two is where the action really begins. The seller will hold center stage for the first part of this meeting. *Just listen.* Don't react. And don't be surprised if you hear anger. It's common, and it's normal. After all, you're talking about his baby. Illogical as it may seem, the seller sees the world very differently from you. Think about how biased your views are about those things that are very important to you, and you'll have some idea of how the seller feels about the business.

Simply refuse to fight. Let him blow off steam. No matter how difficult this is for you, don't get into an argument. This is not a debate. There's no right or wrong. Your view of the deal looks as preposterous to him as his does to you. Your goal at this point is to identify the issues that need resolution. Therefore, after he's laid out a counterproposal, clarify anything you don't understand.

Then say something like, "Thank you for letting me know exactly where you stand. You know, I didn't realize what an emotional roller coaster ride this would be for both of us. But then, this is pretty important to both of us, isn't it? As a starting point, I'd like to go through our proposals together and see where we agree and where we disagree. Does that make sense to you?"

Now you've accomplished two things. First, he realizes that his emotional reaction is not to you but to the situation and that it's perfectly normal. This allows him to save face and continue with the negotiations. Second, you've agreed on a strategy to get the ball rolling toward an agreement.

Once you've identified where you are both in agreement and you've isolated the issues that need to be negotiated, it's a good idea to point out that perhaps you're closer together than you originally thought. Then start by resolving the easy issues, saving the hardest for last. This creates an atmosphere of solid progress, and you'll invariably uncover information you can use in later negotiations.

Once the easy issues are behind you, define the nitty-gritty issues that still must be resolved. Shift the focus from attacking one another to attacking the problem. Ask the seller: "How can we create a solution we both can live with?" Successful negotiation lies in understanding what the other side wants and finding a way to get as close to it as possible. This is a good point to wrap up this session. Agree to go away and think about how you can make progress toward resolving the issues you've identified.

Do you see what's happening here? You're eliminating the adversarial relationship that torpedoes most deals. Instead, you're asking the seller to help you figure out how to do this deal to your mutual benefit. You're drawing him into a problem-solving mind-set and giving him a stake in the outcome. You're together on the same side of the table working on the problems.

Refining the Strategy

Before your next negotiation session, meet with your advisers and brainstorm options for resolving the key issues. Invent as many options for mutual gain as you can possibly think of. The more ways you can give the seller to say yes, the more likely you will be to reach an agreement.

Focus on the interests of the seller, rather than on his stated position. If you can find a creative way to satisfy his interests, he'll move. Here's an example. Suppose the seller's position is: "I need to clear $500,000 after taxes." His interest is making sure he can make enough money to retire without having to go back to work full-time. Rather than arguing about the purchase price, perhaps you could offer him a long-term consulting contract. He gets the income he needs. You get the tax break and avoid paying up-front cash you can't afford.

Another example. The seller wants $750,000 for the company. Your position is: "I won't pay more than $650,000. The cash flow just can't service the debt on a $750,000 price." Your interest is finding a way to buy the company using the available cash flow. Solution? A longer debt period or a balloon payment to lower the annual debt service.

There are many paths to the same place. As long as you focus on the interests of the parties rather than on their expressed positions, a multitude of creative solutions is possible. Whenever you can, draw the seller into a partnership in which you design solutions to solve mutual problems. These are likely to be creative, satisfying solutions that neither of you would have come up with alone.

Be Reasonable—Do It My Way

In your next negotiating session, start out by recapping the issues on which you've reached agreement. Then get them down on paper. That way neither of you can forget or misunderstand what you've already agreed to, and you can clearly see the progress you've made.

Now attack the major issues. A good strategy is to concede slowly. Always get something in return for a concession, and know its worth. Don't be afraid to state your interests clearly. If the seller has a thorough understanding of the link between your position and your interests, it's easier for him to see the world as you do. And a motivated seller will think of solutions you may have overlooked.

Reason, and be open to reason. The more you can use solid evidence to support your case, the better. The more often you can cite a precedent, the stronger your case. Again, don't be surprised at the emotion on both sides. If things begin to get hot, back off and tackle another issue—preferably one you can make progress on. And whatever you do, don't make threats. A take-it-or-leave-it attitude almost always results in leaving it.

If the seller gets angry and begins to push, don't push back. The ancient art of jujitsu uses the opponent's strength to move him. The same principle is extremely effective in negotiating. Don't defend your ideas; invite criticism and advice. Then recast an attack on you as an attack on the problem. Ask for help in rethinking and shaping a solution.

Keep in mind that *no* is a reaction, not a position. Your job is to get beyond the no to the underlying interests. It's only then that you can suggest a win-win solution.

When you just can't seem to make progress on an issue, cite how others have solved the problem. Sometimes it makes sense to get an outsider to help you reach agreement. The best candidate is a neutral third party. This could be an accountant or attorney who is experienced in negotiating business deals. Ask your personal accountant or lawyer for a referral. Of course, you'll need the seller's approval. Fact finders, as they are called, often get things moving when negotiations seem hopelessly stalled.

Above all, remember this: Someone must lead this dance, and it may as well be you. When you establish the ground rules and take the leadership role, you've stacked the deck in your favor. A great negotiator for the U.S. State Department once said, "Be hard on the problem and soft on the people." When you separate the people from the position and understand their interests, you'll be well on your way to negotiating a deal that works.

Negotiation Guidelines

If you are to negotiate effectively, you must know where you're going and have a strategy for getting there. You must know where you'll bend and where you won't. You must be willing to see things from the seller's point of view. And remember, you are in no position to demand anything. The seller will respond favorably only when she sees your overall deal as favorable.

That means you have to figure out what's the top priority to the seller. Where will she bend and not bend? What seems like a minor issue to you frequently is of major significance for the seller. Conceding that point may give you great leverage to get what's critical for you. Here are some guidelines to keep your negotiations moving toward a desirable outcome.

1. *The stated issue is not always the real issue, and the first offer is never the final offer.* Remember, if you can figure out what the seller's interests are and find a way to help her get what she wants, issues and final offers can change dramatically.

2. *Don't ever waste time negotiating with the wrong person.* Strange as it may seem, many would-be buyers never get the sale to go because they're not negotiating with the person who has the power and authority to cut a deal. If you're not dealing directly with the owner, always ask directly, "Do you have the authority to negotiate this sale?" If not, it's pointless to proceed.

3. *Have the facts to support your case.* If you can document why your position on any issue is rational and reasonable, there's a good chance you can get the seller to see it your way.

4. *Cash is king.* The more up-front cash you can offer, the more power you have to lower the purchase price. Start low, and concede slowly.

5. *A dollar is not a dollar.* The tax laws have a substantial impact on the real dollars the seller will come away with. Ask your professional advisers to devise creative ways of putting more actual dollars in the seller's pocket while minimizing the impact on you.

6. *Create many options to solve a problem.* Work as a team with the seller to dream up as many possibilities as you can. The more choices you have, the better the odds are of finding a good win-win solution.

7. *When under attack, be quiet and listen.* If you retaliate, you'll succeed only in creating hostility. Swallow your pride. Bite your

tongue. Look beyond the anger to what's causing it. If you can find the root, you've found the key to resolving the issue.

8. *Plan your work, and work your plan.* Establish an agenda and a time limit for each negotiating session. Don't wallow around without knowing exactly what is to be accomplished. And remember that the discussion will expand to fill the time available. Don't let a meeting drag on with unproductive discussion.

9. *To resolve a tough issue: Agree on exactly what the problem is.* Gather all relevant data. Restate the problem, integrating the interests of both buyer and seller. Together, brainstorm solutions. Evaluate them and agree on the one that works best for you both. When this technique doesn't work, put the issue aside and tackle others. You'll often find that the answer will come from resolving seemingly unrelated problems. If all else fails, agree on an outside source to help you both see the problem from a fresh angle.

10. *The relationship is everything.* Make it your top priority. If it's bad, all the facts and logic in the world will count for nothing. If it's good, you can move the earth.

It's a lot of work, and emotions often run high on both sides. But if you accept that emotionality as normal, use the strategy outlined here, and truly commit yourself to finding a win-win solution, chances are you'll come away having purchased your dream business.

13

In My Professional Opinion . . .

Getting What You Need From Advisers

Finally finding the business that seems perfect for you is without a doubt one of the most exciting landmarks you'll experience in your career. It's an emotional high. And because you are emotionally charged, you're likely to have an incredibly distorted view of the business. Don't believe it? How objective do you think you are about your kids, spouse, or mother?

No matter how hard you try, your perception is likely to be off the mark. Human nature being what it is, it's likely you're not seeing things that others would see. It's likely you're discounting details that to you seem relatively unimportant, whereas others would attach a great deal of importance to them. You need a reality check. In fact, you need several of them. You're not contemplating buying a second-hand car here. There's too much on the line to make a mistake that could have been easily avoided.

Experienced business buyers place a great deal of emphasis on listening carefully to the opinions of others, particularly those without a vested interest. You'd be wise to find a couple of people whose business judgment you respect and to ask them to take a look at your potential acquisition. Where are they aligned with your views, and where are they not? Wherever you find a discrepancy, the smart thing to do is to subject that issue to more research. Maybe they're wrong and you're right. Maybe not.

Helpful as your professional business acquaintances may be, they're not all created equal. If Uncle George has spent his life in finance, he may have valuable insight regarding financial issues;

169

however, he may not have much to offer regarding whether those sales projections are realistic or pie in the sky. What you don't want is a group of your friends pooling their ignorance. Free advice can be very expensive.

Help From Business Brokers

Let's back up to the beginning for a moment. Remember the discussion about business brokers in Chapter 7? Although you should not rely on brokers as the major vehicle for locating your business, neither should you discount them. It's worth the effort to locate good ones. The real professionals can sometimes lead you to an opportunity that you would never have surfaced on your own.

To locate a stable of broker prospects, check your newspaper and the yellow pages, and ask for referrals from your banker, lawyer, or accountant. Here are some things to keep in mind in selecting one or more brokers to work with:

1. *Bigger is not necessarily better.* Two- or three-person firms that specialize often give the best service. For example, if you're interested in manufacturing, try to find brokers who specialize in that field.

2. *Good brokers always ask two questions: "Do you know what you want?" and "How much money do you have?"* If you don't hear those questions early in your conversation, you're wasting time.

3. *Make the rounds of the brokerage firms in your area.* It's hard to make a judgment on the phone. Once you're face-to-face, it's much easier to separate the sheep from the goats. Are you seeing and hearing the professionalism you'd expect?

4. *Ask the broker about his or her personal business experience.* If he doesn't really have an understanding of business, he won't be taken seriously by the sellers you want to deal with. Don't write off the entire firm yet. Ask to see another broker.

5. *Ask how many companies the brokerage has sold in the last year.* What kind? How many are similar to what you're looking for? This will tell you a good deal about the odds they'll perform for you.

6. *Does the broker provide professionally designed material to give you a good business profile of prospective firms?* If the answer is no, it's an indication of unwillingness or inability to do the required homework. Either way, it's unlikely you'll hit pay dirt here.

7. *If the broker tries to show you what you've said you don't want, give the firm one more chance with another broker before writing it off.*

8. *Once you feel that you're dealing with a competent broker, make him work for you.* He'll do that if he's convinced that you're a serious buyer (many people aren't). Also, the more cash you can put into a deal, the harder the broker will work for you. Good brokers are top salespeople who work hard to create deals for serious buyers and serious sellers. So make sure the broker sees you as a highly qualified buyer.

9. *Don't pay a lot of attention to the brokerage firm's promotional literature.* Brokers, not brochures, make things happen for buyers and sellers.

10. *When you find a good broker, stay on him.* The problem in the brokerage business is the supply side. There are plenty of qualified buyers. You want him to think of you first when he runs across a company that fits your requirements.

11. *Ask for references.* This is no time to be shy. Good brokers have a stable of satisfied clients who will be happy to discuss their experience.

Also, don't forget that business brokers, much like real estate brokers, owe their loyalty to who's paying them: the buyer. The fee (10–12 percent of the sale price), although technically paid by the buyer, is actually paid by the buyer in the form of an inflated sale price.

Your Banker and Other Free Professionals

Although in today's banking environment it's not likely your bank is going to help you buy your business unless the note is heavily collateralized by personal assets, your banker may be a source of valuable information about how to examine a business opportunity with a practiced and dispassionate eye. And that advice is free for the asking.

Many commercial loan officers have just the experience you need to help you evaluate your deal intelligently. Evaluating small businesses, after all, is what they do for a living. Before you approach them, however, have your act together. You need an accurate and detailed description of the company's past, along with financials and your business plan for its future, including a three-year pro forma.

It doesn't matter a whit that you're not asking for a loan. If you're going to be in business, you're going to need a bank to service your business. Bankers understand that you may need a line of credit, a loan against receivables, or maybe capital to grow the business down the road. Simply indicate you'd like to have them service your business should you decide to buy it. Then let your banker look at the opportunity and give you feedback.

There are other free sources of professional advice, seldom used by business buyers. Many states have organizations that exist solely to help entrepreneurs like you. Check with your state's department of economic development or its equivalent. Also check various federal agencies such as the Small Business Association (SBA). Your state university's business school and private business schools are often looking for people like you. Get a copy of the business school's directory that lists names of the faculty, give them a call, and tell them what you want. You'll be pleasantly surprised by the enthusiastic reaction. You may make an excellent practical project, and generally the help you get is pretty darn good.

Your Accountant—Now and Forever

If there's one professional that will be indispensable to the long-term health of your company, it's your accountant. Selecting an accountant to help you manage your business will be one of the most critical business decisions you will make during the start-up phase of operating your new company. Companies often thrive or die solely because of the quality of their accounting practices.

It's equally important that you have that enlightened soul by your side as you decide if and how to purchase your dream. As in any profession, there are those who are highly competent and those who aren't. And it may surprise you to know that many accountants don't have a clue about how to buy a business intelligently. They have had zero training and experience in this area. How do you find the gem and avoid the clunker?

First, check with other businesspeople. The yellow pages is not the way to find someone this critical. You need to find someone with both a proven track record and enthusiastic endorsements from businesspeople. Don't assume, however, just because an accountant gets high marks from businesspeople operating professional service companies, that she'll do as well helping you with your manufacturing company. The two types of businesses are very different, and you will require an expert familiar with the complexities and issues of manufacturing. You wouldn't go to a dermatologist to get that triple bypass operation, would you?

Generally, you can expect accountants to have the bulk of their experience in the following areas: retailing, manufacturing, service, or nonprofit. Ask yourself, "What category do I fall into, and can this accountant service me?" Check to see what percentage of the accountant's client base matches your category. Then ask for several references and check them—not on the phone, in person. You'll be able to get the straight story on what that accountant actually did and how well she did it only if you sit down fact-to-face with her clients. Think about how useless most phone recommendations for job applicants turn out to be.

Explore such questions as: What are the accountant's strengths and weaknesses? Does she help you with more than just keeping track of the numbers for tax purposes? If so, how? Has she helped you save money or make money? How? Above all, check on timeliness. One of the biggest complaints business owners have about their accountants is the accountants don't get critical financial information to them when it's needed. All the financial information in the world is worthless if it's not available when you need it to make business decisions. In other words, be as specific as possible.

If your prospective accountant passes these questions with flying colors, then decide if there's a philosophical match. Is he ready and willing to take the initiative to seek out every legal opportunity to avoid taxes? Is he ready to take on the IRS and aggressively represent your interests? Some are, many are not. If your accountant is ultra-conservative and you're not, you may find yourself at loggerheads more often than you'd like. Not that you want a yes-man. You simply want to be certain that the business views of your accountant align as closely as possible with yours.

Don't be shy about asking about fees. Will you be charged hourly or at a flat rate? Don't make a decision strictly on price. Make it on value received for the price. An accountant who is a strategic part of your business is worth more than someone who simply acts as a bookkeeper.

Should you consider only certified public accountants? Not necessarily. Most small, closely held companies do not require CPAs. A public accountant can often do as well for your small business at less cost. Knowledge and experience, not credentials, are what count.

Last, check carefully to see how much experience your prospect has had in helping people like you buy a company. It may surprise you to know that many accountants have virtually no experience in this area. You can't have someone learning at your expense. Imagine if you were on the operating table and your doctor said, "Hey, great! This is my very first open-heart surgery."

Once you've found an accountant that fits the bill, how do you work with her to analyze thoroughly the prospective business? You can expect your accountant to provide more financial detail than the free advisers we've mentioned. Not only should she be able to tell you what the business is worth, she should also be able to tell you what kind of shape it's in, what you're going to need going in to meet the financial requirements of the company, how you'll meet both the operating costs and the debt service, and, depending on your plans for the company, what kind of money you're going to make and when. And she should have some options and strategies for putting the deal together.

Since your accountant is your key financial adviser in putting your deal together, she should feel comfortable in each of these areas. If she doesn't, beat a hasty retreat and find someone else who does.

That doesn't mean your accountant is responsible for making the decisions. That's your responsibility. You need to be in control. It's your money and your life we're talking about, not your accountant's. And although it's difficult to compile a list of questions that apply to all situations, use the following to help your accountant give you the best possible advice.

Accountant Checklist
1. What process did you use to value the business, and why?
2. Is the cost of sales high or low?
3. Are payables and receivables average for this type of business?
4. Is the cash flow sufficient to handle the debt?
5. Is the business value I've pegged realistic?
6. What's the actual cash thrown off by the business?
7. Should the sale be structured as an asset or a stock sale?
8. How will depreciation affect cash flow over the next five years?
9. Are the operating expenses low or high?
10. Are all operating costs accounted for?
11. What expenses will I incur that are not currently being paid out?
12. How could I cut operating expenses?
13. Is profitability high or low for this type of business?
14. What information do you need that I haven't provided?
15. What improvements should be made in the financial record keeping?
16. What benefits would those improvements produce?
17. Is the long-term debt structured in the best way possible?
18. What will my financial situation look like in three years?

19. What changes should be made in the business? Why? What would be their impact?
20. What arguments can I use to negotiate the best price?
21. How much operating capital will I need initially?
22. What's my break-even point?
23. Is my cash-flow plan accurate?
24. What is profit planning, and how do I do it?
25. Could I generate more profit through better tax planning? How much?
26. How do I construct a three-year pro forma?
27. What financial ratios are important? In this company, are they strong or weak?
28. What can I do to improve the company's overall performance?
29. Is the pricing strategy well-conceived and accurate?
30. What unused debt capacity does the company have?

The Legal Side—Kill All the Lawyers?

Everyone has heard jokes about lawyers. Sure, there are bad lawyers, just as there are bad politicians, doctors, teachers, carpenters, and clergy. And although one might debate whether the incredible amount of litigation in our society and the large number of lawyers is in the public interest, when it comes to buying a business you can't afford to leave home without one.

Selecting Your Lawyer

Like an accountant, a lawyer is a requirement, not an option. If you don't already have a lawyer knowledgeable about buying and selling businesses, you'll have to locate one. The same rules used to select an appropriate accountant apply here. Lawyers specialize. Don't use a divorce lawyer to represent you in buying your business. Be certain you select someone who has logged considerable experience in small-business acquisitions.

You'll want to have your lawyer involved early. Don't wait until you're ready to do the deal. A seasoned veteran can help you craft an investigative approach that ensures you'll uncover problems early and accumulate critical information that will lay the groundwork for developing an effective negotiation strategy.

Buying and selling a business is not only complex; it's fraught with areas where a misstep could prove disastrous. For instance, your attorney will be able to evaluate issues such as product liability and environmental conformance, two issues to take very seriously.

If the purchase of commercial real estate is part of the business you're buying, you need a lawyer who is seasoned in that arena. It's not like buying a house. Checking the title is only a small part of what an expert real estate attorney will do.

Susan Galvin, a commercial real estate attorney who does deals all over the country, observes, "This is no place for amateurs. You can lose everything simply because your adviser made a mistake. The law doesn't excuse you for mistakes or ignorance. When you buy the property, you've also bought any potential liability."

In fact, it's common to find that the existing use of the property is in violation of many local and state requirements. It could cost you plenty to comply with zoning requirements, environmental restrictions, or structural codes regulating substances such as radon, lead paint, and asbestos, as well as method of waste water discharge, and on and on.

"An experienced commercial real estate attorney," says Galvin, "will know what information is critical and how to get it. Insuring yourself against all the potential disasters is prohibitively expensive. If you're buying property where any kind of manufacturing has taken place, be especially diligent. You don't want to have the distinction of purchasing a Superfund site."

There are many other legal issues that can skin you alive if you make a mistake. Never, ever try to be your own attorney when buying a business. It's just plain stupid.

Should Your Lawyer Negotiate for You?

This is a tough one to call. Many lawyers are excellent negotiators. After all, a fair amount of their work is working out deals for their clients. Plea bargaining is a good example. But keep in mind that the legal profession is by its very nature adversarial. The negotiation principles outlined in Chapter 12 are the antithesis of the win-lose philosophy espoused by much of the legal profession.

Some lawyers are aware of the distinction and can change hats not only to represent your interests but also to negotiate effectively with a win-win mind-set. Most cannot. The cause of most complaints from both buyers and sellers in connection with buying or selling a business was the lawyers. The complaints are many. Here are just a few:

"My lawyer irritated the buyer so much that he told me he'd resume negotiations only if I got someone else to represent me."

"Both of us finally realized that our lawyers were serious obstacles to doing the deal. It was as if they saw their primary objective as screwing the other side, rather than finding ways to make the deal work."

"It cost me twice as much in legal fees as it should have because the seller's attorney created unnecessary complexity. Because he was running the clock to the limit, it cost the seller unnecessarily as well. I finally withdrew and bought another company."

Unfortunately, the charge that the lawyers were deal breakers is very common. In their enthusiasm to represent their client's interests aggressively, all too often lawyers kill the deal, rather than moving it to a successful conclusion. The lesson here isn't "kill the lawyers." You need them. But you need to get the buyer to agree that the objective you both should seek is to protect the interests of all parties and negotiate creatively to conclude the deal with both sides feeling like winners.

That means that you make it understood who's working for whom. If you've acted on the suggestions presented in this book, you need have no fear about keeping your lawyer on a short leash. Your attorney is your adviser. It's his role to advise, not to make the decisions.

Experience has shown that the negotiating strategy outlined in Chapter 12 works better than letting the lawyers negotiate the deal. If you have a relationship with the seller, a genuine interest in a win-win deal, and the confidence and the skill to do your own negotiating, your accomplishment will blow the doors off any attempt by lawyers to do the same. It's also considerably cheaper.

But a word of caution. If you're truly not up to the task, have a competent lawyer or other professional negotiate for you. If you plan to do your own negotiating, keep your lawyer informed of every move. And make it very clear that anything you agree to is subject to your lawyer's approval.

Avoiding Sticker Shock

A final word about fees. Before you hire an attorney, sit down and get very, very specific about the fee structure. Much of the trauma associated with sticker shock results from not understanding exactly what is to be done and what fees are to be charged. Make sure you tell your attorney what you want and don't want. He's not a mind reader. Agree on the scope of the work and an estimate of the dollar amount.

Never accept a bill "for services rendered." Make it clear that you expect an itemized statement. Specific services might include: preparing a Purchase and Sales agreement, forming a new corporation, obtaining permits, arranging environmental site evaluation, and performing a real estate title search. The list can be much longer. Just make it clear that you want your attorney to be specific about what you're buying and the cost of each service. That way, you'll avoid unpleasant surprises.

Your attorney can help immeasurably in structuring and negotiating a deal you'll be happy with. But you must think through carefully what you want and communicate that to your attorney so he can help you get it.

Other Professionals You May Need

You may require other professionals, depending on your deal. Environmental engineers for site assessments are one example. In many states they are not required to carry malpractice insurance and are obligated only to pay back the fee you paid them or $50,000, whichever is less, should their errors later get you into trouble. Not much solace should you get hit with a $10 million lawsuit and lose.

In many areas today, if your business plans include expanding the business, you may be required to do an environmental impact study. Issues like spotted owl nesting sites, wetland habitats for rare plants, or the archaeological significance of your property could have a significant impact on your ability to grow the business. You'd better have someone who knows the ropes here.

If there are safety or product liability issues that could have an impact on your decision to buy, you may need an assessment from an industry expert. Since it's not likely you'll have the knowledge to find the most competent people to assist you, it's important to select an attorney who knows who's who in the zoo. It's worth whatever you have to pay.

Part Three of this book contains cases or true stories that reflect lessons learned during the transition to small-business ownership. This is real-world stuff. So read it carefully, and listen to what it's telling you.

Part Three

How It Works in the Real World

14

Manufacturing Companies

Case A: Land & Sea
Case B: New England Barricade

Now that you're grounded in the strategy and technique of making the switch to the world of business ownership, let's take a look at what the experience is actually like. As you'll see from the case studies in Chapters 14 to 17, there is sometimes a gap between theory and practice.

Since the purpose is to be instructional, read with a critical eye. What did these folks actually do to move from thinking about owning a business to actually owning one? What drove their actions? How did their backgrounds contribute? What was the impact of their strengths and liabilities? What was the transition to owning and running the business like? The second time around, what would they do differently? And most important, what lessons can you learn and apply in your own situation?

One of the cases presents the perspectives of both the buyer and the seller. Knowing what the seller is going through and how he or she views the process of "giving up my baby" can help smooth out the rough spots in putting a deal together.

Many people have observed that the hardest step is not the first step but the first step where actual risk is involved. It's one thing to have a great time traipsing about the countryside looking at interesting businesses. It's quite another to put your money where your mouth is. Although the people in each of these businesses exhibit great diversity in interests, background, and personality, it's remarkable to see how consistent they are when it comes to courage.

Of all the qualities necessary to make the transition to small-business ownership, courage is by far the most critical. Without it, most people will not do what is required to make the change. Without it, it's impossible to stick with the business long enough to make a go of it. Without it, innovation and creative problem solving do not happen. Most of all, without it, the life of business ownership is hell.

The cases profiled in Part Three cover a range of companies, from start-ups to franchises and partnerships to small independent companies. Several of the companies are operated by husband-and-wife teams, which is often a double-edged sword. If you are contemplating involving your spouse in running a business, you would be wise to look closely at the experience of these teams.

Whenever the experience of others is summarized or interpreted, the bias of the author inevitably colors the result. In order to create a truly accurate picture of the experience and perceptions of these business owners, a direct interview format has been used.

Getting the facts is only part of the story. Verbatim quotes capture the emotions, beliefs, and feelings that drive individual behavior. How something is said is often as important as what is said. The interview format for the cases that follow is an attempt to place you at the kitchen table with these folks, to hear in their own words what they have learned as they struggled with the task of finding, buying, and operating their business.

Each of the people interviewed here was eager to help you, the reader, profit from his or her experience. One owner commented, "I wish I could have had a book like this, to help me see the rocks and navigate safely. If my story helps just one person avoid serious problems or have a voyage with a little smoother sailing, that's wonderful." Another said, "I want people to understand what the experience is like emotionally, to feel the fear and frustrations as well as the joys."

Any attempt to instruct you about how to find and buy the business that's right for you would be severely lacking if it failed to provide an understanding of the emotions you must face and work through. For many, this is the most critical part of a successful outcome. So pull up a chair, put your feet up, and listen to their stories.

Case A: Land & Sea

Land & Sea designs and manufactures a variety of high-performance marine products for the racing and high-end recreational markets. The company is the leading manufacturer of outboard performance accessories. Speed and performance equipment is also designed for high-performance land vehicles, such as snowmobiles.

The company owns a number of patents, including one for the world's only automatically shifting propeller for recreational boats. Bob Bergeron started the company fifteen years ago and achieved an annual growth rate of 10 percent through a steady stream of new and innovative products.

Bergeron sold the company to Bob MacDonald, an engineer with a degree from Harvard Business School. MacDonald had held equity stakes in several companies where he had assumed a leading role in spearheading growth. The end result was an attractive net worth and a hankering to run his own company.

Question: *What made you decide to buy your own business?*

Buyer: I had worked in venture capital funding and was the third employee in a start-up called Life Line Systems, which developed an emergency response system for the elderly. I started out as president and sole salesperson, building the company to around $8 million, and took it public in a hot market in 1983. A year later I left because of a disagreement with the CEO over the direction of the company.

After that, I did a stint as president and CEO of another small company. We took it from $2 million to $8 million, but ran into problems expanding and had to cut back. I went to work for another venture capital company and eventually left because of a difference of philosophy about the way the company should be run.

At that point I decided to buy my own company. Obviously, independence was important to me. I didn't want to leave another situation because I didn't agree with the business direction and had no power to do anything about it. I wanted a company that I owned and controlled. I didn't want to have someone else determine my destiny.

I also viewed it as the ultimate test of whether you're any good as a business manager. It's easy to hide behind other people, but when you're running your own venture you can't blame anyone else for failure. I guess I needed that. I needed to know that I could make a go of it in my own company.

Building some serious equity was also an important motivation. At the time I thought it would make sense to buy several small companies where you could do the equivalent of leveraged buyouts. Smaller companies were selling at around three to four times cash flow. Leveraged buyout guys were buying things at eight to ten times cash flow, so it seemed like you ought to buy several companies and do quite well financially.

Boy, was I wrong! Once you get into a small company, you find it's necessary to spend tremendous amounts of time to make it successful. They often also require much more money than you imagined. Theoretically, it's a great idea to buy several small companies at an attractive price and leverage them into a big return. In reality, it's extremely difficult to do. Small companies don't manage themselves. Usually, you're it. Without you, there is no management.

Question: *How did you decide on Land & Sea as an acquisition?*

Buyer: I had looked at a number of possibilities through the newspapers and brokers. After looking at Land & Sea, I quickly lost interest in everything else. It had an interesting product line in an industry I found appealing, and a number of those products were producing a steady cash flow that could be used as a base to build from. The torque shift prop was an exciting new product that had tremendous potential to drive future growth of the company.

The other thing I found attractive was that the company had a strong entrepreneurial owner who was technically very talented and wanted to stay with the company. It was clear to me that if I could take over some of the business management responsibilities, this guy could be free to concentrate more of his technical genius on developing a stream of innovative new products.

A slight negative was that the company was well run. There were good controls. Costs were understood; pricing was good. Productivity was high, and waste was low. So there was little opportunity to realize improvements in those areas. The company was breaking even, so if we were going to make money, we'd have to do it through growth.

Question: *In your mind, what were the pluses and minuses of the current owner staying on?*

Buyer: I wanted the current owner to stay on because I wanted to work only part-time in the business. At the time, I was viewing this opportunity more as an investment than as a full-time job. I was already on the boards of several companies, and my goal was to acquire other companies. I had envisioned my role as a business manager/consultant who could supply capital and business acumen. So having Bob stay on was an attractive plus.

Question: *What additional ideas did you have as you were going through your analysis of the company?*

Buyer: In addition to looking at the state of the company, I sat down with Bob, and we did detailed five-year sales projections. We talked about how we could grow the company, and the numbers looked good. It appeared that I could make a good return.

The marine industry had shown steady growth for ten years. Of course, right after I bought the company, the economy collapsed, and the entire industry went into the dumper. By the time we hit bottom, we were down about 50 percent in revenue on our core products. It was the new torque shift prop that not only saved us but allowed us to grow 30 to 40 percent. So while the industry was down 40 to 50 percent, we were actually able to grow. However, since we had geared up to meet much higher projections, we lost money.

I had gone into the deal projecting I'd have to put in about 25 percent more than the purchase price to fuel the growth. I ended up putting in 90 percent more, plus having to raise an equivalent amount from the outside. Considering the disaster for the industry, it's remarkable we did as well as we did.

Question: *Bob, as the seller of Land & Sea, what were your motivations for selling the business?*

Seller: I was coming off a product liability suit that really bothered me. It fueled a great deal of uncertainty. The experience drove home the fact that, even after I'd spent my professional life building the business, I could lose it all. No question, that soured me on continuing as the owner. I realized that product liability would always be a serious problem. Some little product that never contributed much could blindside you at any time. And whether you won or lost was a roll of the dice. After just experiencing the absurdity of how the system worked, I wasn't keen on continuing my exposure.

I also had been thinking about growth and realizing that more money would be needed if the company was going to grow. I had also seen a number of acquaintances making big money, not working nearly as hard as I was. I was thinking about all of this when I was approached about the idea of selling the company. Normally, I wouldn't have been interested, but I thought, well, maybe it's time at least to explore the idea of selling out. If I could get a good price, maybe it would be worth it. I wasn't about to be snowed into doing something I didn't want to do.

Question: *What was it like for you going through the selling process?*

Seller: Not easy. In fact, it was agony going through it. It took much more time than I wanted to spend. After a while, I really believed it wasn't going to happen. It was a big relief the day I said, "No, I'm not going to sell." I'm glad that chapter is behind me. Then twenty-four hours later it was back on again.

My accountant was saying, "No way, don't sell." My lawyer was saying, "Watch out for this. Watch out for that." It turned out they were both wrong. What I found attractive and convinced me to stay with it and try to do the deal was that the buyer was an engineer who could appreciate the technical side of the company, as well as the business problems. I was impressed by his business sophistication. If what he seemed to be was actually true, here was a business-person with an engineering background who could provide the leadership the company needed. The whole process beginning to end was stressful.

Buyer: From my viewpoint, there was also emotion; although in my case I had already done many deals as a venture capitalist, so I viewed it as one more deal, rather than as my life savings on the line. As it turned out, it certainly did involve my life savings and became very emotional after the fact. I should have paid more attention at the time.

Question: *Many readers will be confronted with the question of buying a company outright versus going into a partnership with the current owner or keeping the seller on as an employee. How has it been for the two of you working together?*

Seller: It has not been easy for either of us. But the fact that right after Bob bought the business we went into a downturn and he had to put in more money than he had planned and ride out some tough times makes it easier for me to accept it when he makes some big money. He's paid his dues. Perhaps I could have ridden it out alone, but perhaps I would have gone under.

If it turns out that he makes $30 million now, I won't feel that's my money he stole. He's earned it.

Buyer: We originally structured the deal so that Bob would be able to buy back some of the company. I don't know how much that meant to him at the time, but it could mean a great deal later on. And even though I'm here full-time and he's not managing the company the way he used to, I've tried to keep him involved in the key decisions. Since from the beginning it was always my intention to keep Bob involved in the company long term, I've tried to structure the deal so he'd want to stay.

But we've had some rough times in terms of our personalities and figuring out how to work together. I think Bob thought I'd be able to offer more in terms of improving operations than I actually could.

Question: *What advice do the two of you have for people who are contemplating becoming involved in situations where the seller stays on?*

Seller: You have to go in expecting that it's going to take time to work out an effective working relationship. You're immediately thrust into a situation that requires working together without the trust that time brings. It's natural to look for ulterior motives. You're thrown into a foxhole together. It's like a new marriage, only worse. There's going to be a period of adjustment.

In our situation, we didn't communicate as well as we should have. I was now in a different role. Decisions that I had made for years were no longer mine. I looked at what he did and said and concluded that whatever he does must be magic, or it must be the way big companies do it, or he must know what he's doing. In the beginning we spent a lot of money simply experimenting. That really sucked up cash.

Buyer: I think the truth is that we were both extremely honest with each other, but it's only over time that you actually know that. Over time we both realized that we were both trying our damnedest to do what was best for the business. We came to realize there were no hidden agendas. If there had been, it would have killed any working relationship. And most important, we have come to realize that the company is far stronger because the two of us are both in it.

We both have very different and necessary skills. It's so tough to have all the brains you need in a small company. Bob has frequently kept me from making mistakes because I don't have the history and experience he has. My biggest contribution to the company was bringing money.

Question: *What was actually going through negotiating the deal like for each of you?*

Seller: My biggest thing was coming down in my asking price to a place where I could feel I could sell and wasn't giving my business away. And since I didn't know the buyer, there was a lack of trust. That's why I went to a cash deal and wouldn't hear of anything else. My accountant, lawyer, wife, and common sense all pushed me in that direction. Other areas were negotiable.

Buyer: Looking back, I can't think of anything I would have done differently. Perhaps someone in the industry could have had a sense that things were starting to slow down. It was tough analytically to figure that out.

Like Bob, I went against all professional recommendations also. The professionals tell you not to buy stock. Buy the assets so you don't get stuck with the corporation's liabilities or other bogeymen that can come out of the closet years later. Try not to pay cash up front. In my case, however, it was the only way the deal was going to get done. At some point you decide whether you want it or not, and I did.

I felt that Bob was honest and telling me everything he knew, and, therefore, if it turned out that there was a mistake of $10,000 or $20,000 in inventory, payables, or receivables, it didn't matter one way or the other.

Seller: The fact that he was willing to include that in the agreement probably did more than anything else to convince me that I was dealing with an honest straight shooter that I'd be able to work with. I was worried about what would happen if later on we find out that through a bookkeeping error or something we're $5,000 short on receivables or some inventory is found to be unusable. He eliminated that worry without my even asking.

Buyer: This deal never would have happened if we had allowed lawyers to negotiate and do all the paperwork for us. We could not have settled our differences through them. Lawyers always look at all the contingencies, no matter how remote. What happens is that they sometimes create an adversarial climate where the deal is the victim.

Seller: I kept a tight rein on my lawyer. It's true, they're always looking for reasons not to go ahead. Ultimately, if a deal is going to go you've got to work with the buyer and decide if your trust level is high enough to go ahead.

Buyer: We didn't have a disagreement in our negotiations where one of us couldn't give in because we were both trying to be reasonable. And since neither one of us was trying to screw the other or looking for an improved position over the other, we were able to keep moving ahead without a lot of conflict.

Seller: I couldn't agree more. I felt that we were both looking to find a way to do the deal so that we both could feel good about the outcome. It surprised me that he was genuinely concerned about me. It impressed me enough to work toward closure.

Question: *What was the final deal you negotiated?*

Buyer: I paid cash up-front for 100 percent of the stock. Bob got a five-year employment agreement and stayed on as president. He also had an option to buy back up to 20 percent of the stock at escalating prices. There was also a bonus arrangement based on meeting certain business objectives.

Seller: The whole deal happened in less than two months. The only thing that held it up was that the banks were in trouble everywhere, and it took a while for Bob to get the money he needed. He ended up having to put up his house.

Question: *What was the actual closing like?*

Seller: It was anticlimactic. The details had all been settled, and I was anxious to get it over. We were coming into our busy season, and I had to know one way or the other. I would be executing a different plan if Bob didn't buy, and I needed time to put the pieces in place. Since we both knew exactly what was going to happen the next business day after the closing, there were no unknowns.

Buyer: I would agree. The closing was simply directing the lawyers to do what we had agreed to. The pressure, at least relating to the sale, was over at that point.

Question: *What advice would you have for others buying their first business about the transition to new ownership?*

Seller: Realize that a lot can go wrong. The risks are very real. I continue to be impressed that we pulled it off and that it's working. Also realize it's hard for the seller as well as the buyer. If you're holding a note or you're employed with the company as I am, you worry about the company stumbling under new leadership.

What if the industry goes south as it did in our situation? The buyer is green. What kind of problems could result? If you can put yourself in the seller's shoes, it will be easier to get his concerns out where you can deal with them.

Buyer: Realize that it will take you a minimum of a year to learn the business. Mistakes can cost customers and money. A big mistake could cost you the business. The classic problem of not being able to fund the company once you've bought it is a very real one. You'll end up putting in much more than you'd originally planned on.

Realize that things take time. One of the things I didn't understand going in was how long it takes to initiate change. People need time to adjust. I underestimated the stress the change in ownership would place on the employees. Even now there's still resentment and mistrust. My advice would be to smoke out those problems early and think through how to deal with them effectively. If you ignore them or let them fester, it just gets worse. For me, this has been the most unpleasant part of taking over the business.

Question: *What was the scariest part of doing a deal like this?*

Buyer: The smoking gun. It's buying the time to get the business under control. What could go wrong in that period that you didn't anticipate or that you don't have the ability to deal with? It's probably a two- or three-year time period before you know for sure how to run the business. The danger is what can go wrong during that shakedown period. Uncertainty diminishes with experience. Knowing that your inexperience may be your undoing is certainly scary.

Question: *How has working together after the sale of the company been different from what you thought it would be?*

Buyer: The biggest thing by far has been dealing with the people issues. I guess that's a risk associated with keeping the previous owner on as a significant force in the business. Even while Bob and I were able to work through our adjustment period, the fact that he's here creates issues we must deal with.

There have not been any serious business problems that surfaced. The downturn in the economy was terrible, but we made it through because of the strengths that attracted me to the company in the first place. It was a mistake to invest more money before I understood the business. I added substantial overhead during the first three months. Changing the overhead structure rapidly was a mistake. We would have been okay if the economy had helped, but it didn't.

I also didn't realize how much of my time and energy would have to be invested. It required more money as well. I'm not sure how much of that I could have foreseen, but it certainly bears more careful consideration than I gave it.

It's interesting. In all my experience with the venture capital firms and my personal ventures, I've yet to see a company follow its business plan. Not that you don't need one. You need to know where you're headed and how you're going to get there, but it's surprising how much is determined by your ability to read what's happening right now and to react immediately. Luck will always be a factor. You'll experience both good luck and bad luck. The trick is to figure out how to ride out the bad luck and to seize the opportunity that the good luck presents. No matter how well you plan, it never turns out exactly the way you thought it would.

Question: *What's been the upside and the downside of working together?*

Seller: I've learned a good deal from having a real peer in the business, really for the first time. It's been a real plus. It's so tough to get that in a small company.

Buyer: Although I own the business now, I view Bob as a partner in the business. I guess I believe it's developing into a partnership. Maybe Bob doesn't quite believe that and I probably don't act like it some of the time, but it's becoming obvious that it's the best way to get the results we want.

Seller: When I was the boss, I thought I had an accurate read on where employees are. Now that I'm more like one of them, they confide in me more. It's amazing what I didn't know. I never realized how much employees see their fate and livelihood as being in the hands of their boss.

When Bob bought the business, there was this expectation that, here's Santa Claus and he's going to instantly bring magic to the company. I'd say that I had some of that feeling as well. When that didn't happen, it was disappointing. The reality is, here's a guy working hard to make the company successful.

Buyer: Success usually comes from lots of little things, not something major.

Seller: All that stuff you read about in the management books about preparing people for change and introducing the changes slowly is true. Even if the changes are needed and will be great for the company, there will be resistance simply because it's a new idea.

It was incredible how much I wouldn't hear because I was looking for a hidden agenda. It was the same with other employees. It wasted a lot of time and energy.

Buyer: Frequent and totally honest communication is so important. Because we were immediately caught up in the hundreds of details of running the business, we didn't communicate as well or as often as we should have. The required relationship will not just happen. You have to make it happen. It's as important as anything else you do—probably more.

It's fortunate we were physically in the same office. It facilitated some critical communication that might not have happened.

Seller: I think that perhaps the most important part of buying a business is paying attention to doing whatever you can to plan an orderly transition to the new ownership. Bob didn't really do anything wrong. Unfortunately, you need time to build the trust required to realize there are no ulterior motives.

Question: *Any final advice for would-be buyers?*

Seller: I really believe you have to be clear about why you're buying a business. I've read in so many business books that the purpose of a business is to make a profit. Maybe for big business, but for a small business that's baloney. It's to make the owner happy. Ask yourself, would you take a new job that makes you miserable just to increase your salary by 25 percent? I wouldn't.

The question, then, is this: Is the business you're considering going to make you happy?

Buyer: I'd agree. You work too hard. There's got to be more than monetary reward. If you approach the decision from a purely logical point of view, you'll never do it. The emotional element has to be there. Owning and running a small business is not all roses. There will be some tough times, and it's your resources on the line. But it's never boring, and the potential for great reward is what makes it attractive.

We've gone through some tough times with the market and we've gone through a period of adjustment. But we're now getting to the fun part. The potential here is very exciting.

Case B: New England Barricades

New England Barricades manufactures and sells construction barricades, signs, and other safety products mainly to municipalities and highway construction contractors. In business for twenty-seven years, it was recently bought by Warren Frank, an engineer who has spent thirty-five years in manufacturing organizations, including Eastman Kodak, New Britain Machine, and the Stanley Works. After losing several jobs, he decided to look seriously for a business of his own. Armed with an MBA from Wharton and his thirty-five years in the trenches, he began his search for a small manufacturing company.

> "I began to realize that having my job eliminated was going to be a continual reality in today's world. Performance and loyalty were becoming less and less important. It was time to control my own destiny. Realizing that I was no spring chicken and that the job market was tight and likely to remain so, the most attractive alternative seemed to be owning my own business.

"My wife and I talked about it for some time. I think it's important for people reading this to be aware of how important it is to have the support of your spouse. It's a very trying period to go through. Since it's likely to take a while to find the right business, it's a drain on funds. If you're serious, it's a 110 percent commitment. When you actually start running your business, the hours will be long. And there's always the possibility you may lose everything you've put into the company. If there are children involved, it's even more of a strain. It can be a hard time emotionally. If your relationship is not strong, you could be in trouble.

"I started my search with research. I read every book I could find on the subject of how to buy a business. I talked with brokers, finally finding an excellent firm that I worked with for two years. I spent so much time with them that they finally asked me to go to work for them, which I did for six months. That really gave me access to a lot of opportunities before they became known to everyone.

"Through that exposure, I identified three companies to explore. One was a pewter manufacturing business. That interested me because of my metalworking and manufacturing background. After looking at it, I felt it was just too sensitive to the ups and downs of the economy. What's interesting is that it fit perfectly with my interests and experience, but it was strictly a luxury item.

"The second business was a laundry, a profitable stable business with a reliable customer base. The problem there was it would not meet environmental standards. That's a problem for many businesses today. You have to be alert to the EPA issues and investigate carefully. I paid to have a site assessment done. It failed. To bring the company up to standard was too expensive.

"The third business was this one. I had examined the financials in detail before the first visit. Since the business was healthy and doing well, my first question was, "Why are you selling?" The seller owned several other companies, and he was getting heavily involved in another venture that required a heavy time commitment.

"Since the seller owned several companies and the operating expenses were not separated, it was necessary to recast the financials to reflect the true picture more accurately. He owned a number of vehicles that were used by several of his companies. Insurance was a chore to sort out. Also, there were things like the fact that he owned the building that housed the business and was not charging the company for rent. The business broker helped a lot with that.

"I had questions about the labor costs. I discovered that they were probably higher than they needed to be. There were questions about make versus buy and about the inventory value. It seemed high. What did the inventory value actually reflect in terms of materials? How much was actually usable?

"The seller was great. He was very open. He didn't hide anything. He took me through every aspect of the business. I got a good feel for the products and for how the company operated.

"As I was assessing him, he was doing the same with me. I realized I had to pass certain tests if he was to feel comfortable selling the company to me. He made it clear that he wanted assurances that the business would continue to be successful and not be run into the ground. I guess we met four times. The second meeting was to answer questions about my background so that he could decide if I was capable of running the company competently.

"The third meeting was a discussion of the financial part of the deal—how much I could put up front, how much a bank might fund, how much he would take in paper, and so forth. I expect he had my credit checked so that by the fourth meeting we were prepared to deal. I had a concern about what I considered excess inventory. He agreed to what I considered a reasonable total; he would retain the rest. If I needed it later, I could repurchase it at the same price I sold it to him for. I presented an offer that was essentially his asking price.

"Of course, all through this process, I was doing a lot of research, and the broker was back and forth sorting out issues. The seller agreed he'd sell the assets of the company, no stock. He agreed to take his paper as a covenant not to compete, allowing me a good tax advantage. He also agreed to stay with me to help me learn the business, to introduce me to customers, and to sell the employees on the deal.

"I researched the industry, logging a good deal of library time in trade journals and other publications to get a feel for the key industry problems and issues and to scout the competition. I discovered that by automating, I could cut some material costs and substantially lower labor costs. That made the financial picture even more attractive.

"My research showed that the market was not heavily dependent on the economy. Roads fell apart and needed repair regardless of the current economic situation. And municipalities, which account for 50 percent of the business, are extremely sensitive to litigation these days. They replace missing or damaged signage quickly. Contractors are being subjected to more regulation regarding signage. It looked like not only a stable market but a growing one.

"In doing my research on New England Barricades, I found it to be a great little company. The customers were happy, and 90 percent of the business was repeat business. The product was easy to manufacture, with little risk environmentally. The bad debt was very low, and the state even helps out in getting paid. They require signage to conform to regulations before the job starts. They also require sign-off from the contractors' vendors before the final payment is released. So if I'm not getting paid, all I have to do is petition the state and the contractors suddenly become very attentive to paying me. I saw that as a real plus in the business.

"We agreed on a very favorable five-year lease and settled myriad details with little conflict. The seller was willing to back me with his own balloon loan amounting to 60 percent. I also was able to get a seven-year SBA loan for the value of the inventory. I came up with about a third of the purchase price.

"One interesting sidelight. The seller was using a lawyer who insisted on making things more complicated than they needed to be. Because we had a relationship, the seller and I were able to work out problems without the lawyers. Lawyers are important, but it's important to let them know who they're working for and that the job is both to protect the parties and to get the deal done. Lawyers can really blow the deal if you don't control them.

"Overall, putting the deal together progressed very smoothly. Even the bank loan wasn't too tough. I went to the seller's bank. He used them for all of his companies. They knew the business well, and he, of course, had leverage because he did so much of his business there.

"The closing was anticlimactic except for the emotional element. I realized everything I'd saved for my whole life was on the line. One of my first priorities as the new owner was to make sure the employees were feeling good about the change. I knew I'd be dead if they decided to leave. I spent a lot of time talking with them to assure them they would have a job and would have input into any changes.

"I then quickly computerized and bought some computerized equipment to improve business management and the manufacturing process. I've just completed the first year in business. And I'm pleased with the result. Now that I know what my true costs are, the second year will be better. I know how to cost, buy, and price.

"Running the business has been fun. I don't mind working twelve-hour days when it's mine. Sure, I used to be concerned about profit and loss when I was a manager for someone else. But when it's your money, I've noticed you get very interested in every aspect of the business. You watch anything that costs money very carefully.

"I enjoy being a big fish in a small pond. The sense of control, the lack of bureaucracy, and the freedom to respond quickly are pluses. I've discounted a lot of my management training and education. Big companies go overboard on time-motion studies, making jobs incredibly and unnecessarily boring. My employees get a chance to do a variety of jobs.

"I'd never go back to working for someone else. It was not easy making this transition, but it's worth it. As I was going through my long search, I became concerned about becoming a professional procrastinator. You can always find a good reason not to buy a business. It's easy to focus on what's wrong. You get to the point where all you can see is the negative side. It's also easy to become a professional researcher, continuing to generate much more information than needed to make an informed decision. You can get wrapped up in so much irrelevant detail that you lose sight of the goal. What it all boils down to is you're putting off making a decision. No business is perfect. You can always say, "I'll just wait for another opportunity and take a look."

"What I did was set a time frame. I gave myself a generous two years. I was fortunate enough to have enough cash to live for that period of time and still have enough to put into the business.

"Two final thoughts. One, I would caution anyone looking at buying a business, especially a manufacturing business, to look very carefully at the environmental history and what the future holds in terms of being in compliance with the law. Many businesses are virtually unsellable. Look very deep to see if it's dirty.

"Second, work hard on developing the right kind of relationship with the seller. In many cases you need him or her after the sale. Sellers also have concerns about getting paid long-term. Get the issues out and talk about them. In my case, I found that a friend of the seller had sold a business, only to find out that the buyer of that business sold off the inventory and then bailed out, leaving him holding the bag. We legally agreed that whenever my inventory fell below a certain level I would immediately inform him. That resolved a key concern for him. He was just as cooperative about my concerns. If you've got a relationship, it's possible to find a solution to almost any problem."

15

Service Firms

Case A: Anne Holliday & Associates
Case B: Goose Cove Lodge

Case A: Anne Holliday & Associates

Anne, a transplanted Floridian, has bought several professional accounting practices. She began her career as the finance manager for a start-up environmental consulting firm at the ripe old age of twenty. During her tenure she learned on the job how to deal with complex tax situations, the SBA loan process, and the black art of cash-flow management in a small, fast-growing company.

While working full-time for the consulting firm, she also attended school full-time and was licensed as a CPA. As the company grew, her aversion to the cultural realities of larger companies and the predictable routines convinced her it might be time to move on. When the firm was bought by a larger company, she knew it was time.

After a consulting stint with a construction company, Anne was introduced to the owner of a small accounting firm.

> "I never seriously thought about the route many accounting graduates take—going to work for a large CPA firm—although I did interview with one. After they told me they didn't like my liberal attire and that I would be required to dress like a mortician, I said, 'Naw, this isn't for me.'
>
> "To apply for licensing as a CPA, the state requires two years' experience with a CPA firm. I decided it would be a good place to hang out. After I had been working there for only a few months, the owner said he wanted to get out of

the business and wouldn't it be great if I bought the business? My God, I was terrified at the thought. But after the terror subsided, I said, "Well, why not? What's the worst thing that could happen?"

"As it turned out, plenty. But at the time I thought, Well, I have two choices here—hit the streets and look for a job or go along with this foolishness. I decided to give it a shot. I was somewhat familiar with the client list, and although I didn't know the owner well, I didn't see any problems.

"I just followed his lead and let him structure the deal. We went through the client list and placed billing values next to each account. He kept the good accounts. I was given the dogs. He kept the accounts that paid their bills.

"The initial sale agreement was that as cash was received, the former owner would get 25 percent of the gross revenue. I would also be responsible for 80 percent of the rent, the copier lease, and all the other business expenses. I was so naïve. It never even occurred to me to ask these questions: How long was he going to get the 25 percent? What am I actually buying here? How good is this client base I'm purchasing? How much money will I gross? How much will I net? What problems could arise?

"But at the time, I thought, I'm young, inexperienced, and without a client base. Here's an experienced professional willing to give me a good start. I can rely on him for help if I need it. How bad can it be?

"I called a CPA friend, took him to lunch, and asked him his opinion of the deal. He told me point-blank, 'If you do this you're a blithering idiot. You're getting screwed.' Not only did I disregard good advice, but I also didn't retain an attorney to represent my interests.

"So the seller got 25 percent free and clear. He also insisted on seeing my deposit slips daily so he would know if I was cheating him. Out of the 75 percent that I retained, I had to cover the business overhead. What was left over was mine. So off I went into my first tax season.

"I was working day and night and wasn't making a dime. In April I sat down with the seller and told him that I was not happy. So he worked out an elaborate Purchase and Sales Agreement that basically said that I would pay him $55,000 for the practice at the rate of $1,500 a month. There was also a noncompete agreement that prevented me from doing business with the clients he had retained. I was to also pay him a $75-per-hour consulting fee when I needed help.

"By the end of April, we had an agreement. In May, he wanted to sell me one of his better accounts. It was auditing work. The arrangement was that I would take over the account, and, out of the gross received, I was to give him 40 percent. Out of the remaining 60 percent, I had to pay payroll for the auditing staff and cover the business overhead—not a very good way to make money. Over the next year or so, I picked up five or six more clients that he sold to me.

"As time went on, I discovered that many of the clients were in fact not clients. They were unhappy and had no intention of continuing business with the firm. The billings turned out to be much less than expected. Unfortunately, the reputation of the firm turned out to be much less than I had thought.

"And there were other things, like billings but no cash. One client even had an arrangement whereby he would be billed for work and, if he got an SBA loan, then he would pay. During my presale investigation I did examine the client billings to verify that what the seller said was true. But I looked only at the billings, not at what cash was coming in against the billings. Stupid? Yes. But I was so inexperienced. Had I known the questions to ask or at least had competent professional help, none of this would have happened.

"In 1989, when I became licensed as a CPA, I changed the name of the firm. I kept praying for the day when it would be all over. Over the last couple of years I've paid out over $80,000 for a business that was worth a fraction of that.

"In 1989 I bought a tax practice. As a result of my first buying experience, I was much more careful. I actually reviewed the files of clients so that I had a historical picture of each client. We sent out a transition letter informing the customers of the change in ownership. The following week, my secretary spent a day on the phone calling those clients. There was not one negative comment, and the vast majority were comfortable enough to stay on.

"The Purchase and Sales Agreement was simple. Her first proposal was 30 percent of gross billings. We negotiated and settled on a figure of 25 percent of billings of her tax clients for a period of one year. It has turned out to be great for both the seller and me. I'm convinced that the way to grow is to acquire other firms. It's easier and cheaper. I'm currently looking for other practices to buy.

"There are many lessons here, both for myself and for the clients I counsel. I can now see the problems at fifty paces. First, check everything. Don't hang your fate on someone's word. Check the facts for yourself. And remember, you'll get only some of the facts from the seller. You're responsible for uncovering what they'd just as soon you not know.

"Never pay cash. You want the seller holding paper. Usually the tax advantage for the seller of holding paper is greater than that for getting cash up front. So if the seller is not willing to do so, watch out. You have little leverage if things don't turn out to be the way they were painted.

"There are lots of ways to cook the books. Balance sheets and P&Ls are critical, but you should really have someone who's seasoned help you sort out the real story.

"People often think there's a hard and fast process for valuing a small business. There isn't. I often ask a client what he's willing to pay and then use the numbers to either support the price or show why it's not worth it. Sellers will often tell you that the gross revenues are understated. There's a lot of cash not reported. Maybe it's true, but how do you know? Pay for what can be proven, not cash under the table. By the way, though, businesses like pizza shops often do gross twice as much as reported.

"I always counsel my clients to check the company reputation carefully. Whenever possible, go directly to the customers. They'll tell you the truth. If the name is dirt, that goodwill you're buying is worthless.

"Buying a business is serious business. Often there's a lot to lose if it goes sour. Since I wasn't investing a lot of cash up front, I didn't take buying my business as seriously as I should have. I was lucky. It could have turned out to be a nightmare.

"If you're careful and do it right, the joy of owning your own business is incomparable. Every day when I drive up and see my name on the building, I smile."

Case B: Goose Cove Lodge

Joanne and Dom Parisi bought the lodge in 1992. In operation since 1948, it consists of over seventy acres of heavily forested woodlands with miles of hiking trails and spectacular ocean views. The lodge, complete with thirteen buildings, includes twenty-one guest units scattered around the property that house from two to six people each. When full, the property can accommodate up to seventy guests. The business is operated seasonally from May through October.

Joanne's work background includes nearly a decade in the healthcare field and eight and a half years owning and operating a restaurant and a highly successful catering business with twenty-three employees.

Dom spent twelve years as a science teacher. During the mid-1970s he got involved in the energy conservation field. Building on his teaching background, he developed courses and trained energy auditors. As the field took off during the energy crunch, Dom's career took off with it. During his sixteen years in the field he held a variety of management jobs, culminating in the role of executive director and president of an energy organization with 170 employees.

Question: *When did you first start thinking about leaving the energy firm and the catering business to buy a country inn?*

Joanne: We felt that our jobs were creating havoc with our personal lives. Every day we left in opposite directions. I was commuting sixty-five miles a day each way. Dom was logging about the same amount of travel time each day. It was a very fragmented existence. Over time we began to realize this was not the way we wanted to continue living.

Dom: Both our careers were so demanding. Joanne worked nearly every weekend. We had hardly any time together. It got so we actually had to schedule a date to see each other.

It was only on vacation that we really got to spend any time together. One of the things we decided to do was to take longer vacations. In 1989 we took our first two-week vacation ever.

Our interest in innkeeping actually dates back about ten years. It really started when we stayed at a friend's condo at the Killington Ski Resort in Vermont. While there we spent time just going from inn to inn. We'd have lunch at one, dinner at another. We began exploring more inns throughout New England.

We saw some wonderful places and began to think. "Wow, this is really pretty neat!" Compared to the existence we were leading, it seemed very attractive.

Joanne: As our interest grew, we actually started looking. We looked at several properties, but they had no existing business to create the necessary cash flow. We looked at one that had been closed for five years. It was a wonderful place but needed a lot of work, and without ongoing business it would be essentially a start-up.

One of the things I'd learned from starting a catering business is that it takes five years to establish a market. You have to have very deep pockets for a start-up. Then through friends we heard about Goose Cove Lodge.

We learned that the innkeeper's wife had recently died and that the place was for sale. So we drove up to see it. The weather was terrible, but we hiked the trails and talked with the staff and the innkeeper. Instantly, we fell in love with the place. We expressed some interest and then went home.

In mid-August 1990, we had a phone call from the manager, who said they had just let their cook go and were in desperate need of someone who could finish out the month. It was the busiest time of the season, and she wanted to know if Joanne could come up and fill in for two weeks.

The innkeeper said, "If you're really interested in innkeeping, this is your chance to find out if this is what you really want to do. You can get to see the business firsthand."

Even though we'd had our vacation, we thought, "This is an opportunity that is only going to come once. Let's do it." We called back and said we could do a week and she said okay.

Question: *You acted decisively and quickly. Were you scared?*

Joanne: This is where the opportunity we had been seeking opened up. The moment of decision was right there at that point. Neither one of us could afford to take more time off, but I knew we stood at the threshold. You have opportunities in life, and sometimes you don't recognize they're gone until it's too late. I just knew without question that when that phone call came, we had to act or it would be lost forever.

Dom: It forced us to say, "Gee, if we're serious about doing this, we have to act now." They offered to show us everything we could absorb in a week. We could see the entire operation and meet and talk with the guests. So we agreed, if we were serious about this kind of change in our careers, this was the only way we were going to get enough momentum to follow through.

We arrived at noon on a Sunday. There was virtually no food at the place. Joanne had a gourmet meal prepared for sixty people by that evening. The guests loved it. It had been two to three years since Joanne had been in the kitchen.

That same week they fired their maintenance man. I had brought up a bag of tools. I spent a lot of time working on the property, shingling a cottage, fixing windows. We also had a chance to talk with a lot of people about the place and what they liked about it.

I had brought up my computer, and at night I'd sit and work on a business plan. We also got off the property and toured the area, finding out what businesses were in the area and talking with people who ran other inns. We asked what the perception of Goose Cove Lodge was. Among other things, we learned that everyone thought the site was spectacular and the food mediocre. We did a lot of reconnaissance. It was a busy, busy week.

We worked hard getting the business plan together because our intention was to go to local banks before the week was over so that we could get a feeling from them about whether they would have any interest in financing if we became the owners.

Joanne: We were really leading with our hearts, rather than our heads, at this point. Even though we were doing all this research, our emotions were running high. It was hard to stay focused on the facts and make sure it made good business sense to buy.

Dom: I remember the exact moment I became convinced this was right. It was Tuesday evening. The sunset was gorgeous. The weather was perfect. An elderly woman who was unable to get around the property much was sitting on a bench just outside the dining room. She was just watching the sun set over the ocean. I sat watching her. It was one of the most peaceful moments I can remember. Even with all the other positive things we had learned and the great feedback we had been getting from guests that gave us a sense of what the place was all about, the most poignant moment of the week for me was just watching this lovely old lady enjoying the serenity of the place.

In my mind at that very moment I knew this was something I really wanted to do.

Joanne: The moment of truth for me was that foggy day in July when we saw the place for the first time. It may sound corny, but it was as if the land was speaking to me. I felt like I had come home. Certainly, we had to justify the business reasons for buying the business. But it was the emotional commitment that really sold us.

We spent a considerable amount of time listening to what the guests wanted. They did not want big changes. They liked the rustic nature of the place. They didn't want a lot of scheduled activities. No phones or televisions. We read the guestbooks and learned a lot.

Dom: Several guests said, "Look, we are very concerned that the right people buy and run this place and we like you; we feel you're the people who will continue to run the place the way we want it run. If you need some help financially, we will help you."

Joanne: Isn't that unbelievable? To say the least, we were incredibly impressed. And many of the guests expressed this fierce loyalty. A large number had been coming every year for five, ten, fifteen years. About half the guests are repeat customers.

Dom: So by Friday of that week, with business plan in hand, we went off to the banks. One of the banks—in fact, the bank that the previous innkeeper had done business with—expressed interest in financing on the order of $1 million or so. Encouraged, we told the owner we were seriously interested and would get back to him with an offer. The property had been appraised, and we knew what his asking price was.

So we went home with financial statements for the last two years to put together a pro forma. The owner and his bookkeeper were very open about sharing the financials. We worked hard on analyzing where the revenue was coming from and what the expenses were. We created a twelve-month budget and tried to project future costs. From what the owner showed us for the last two years, it looked very profitable.

On the basis of that and what we thought we could do with the place ourselves, we came up with a debt figure we felt the business could support if everything went according to plan. Since we had a limited amount of cash to put in, we had to try to figure out how to finance it. If the bank and the owner would cooperate and we could get an acceptable interest rate, the deal was doable.

So we made an offer that turned out to be far less than the owner was looking for. Since we felt there was little room for us to go higher, we began to lose hope.

Question: *Did you have a commitment from the bank at this point?*

Dom: No, what we had was an expression of interest that seemed pretty solid. In fact, the loan officer indicated that they might be willing to finance the whole thing.

We weren't sure where we could come up with the 20 to 25 percent down payment that would be required.

The owner came back with a number of issues and concerns. For example, he wanted a parcel of the seventy acres reserved for conservation. He also wanted to reserve a parcel in the middle of the property for himself. There were issues as to who would be responsible for problems with the facilities' meeting code, the condition of the septic system, and so on.

We went back and forth on a number of other issues and finally came back with a second offer. It was rejected without a counteroffer. So we figured the deal was dead.

Joanne: That was December of 1990. We had spent about six months pursuing it, and we were still hundreds of thousands apart. We made it clear that it wasn't that we didn't think the business wasn't worth what he was asking but, rather, based on our situation, we couldn't make the deal work. As it turned out, I think that was an important message to send.

Dom: Six months went by. We were vacationing in the area, and, since we were still longing for the place, we decided to stop by and visit. We had heard that it had been sold. We talked with the innkeeper and manager and had a great visit.

Right after we got home, we received a call from the owner's agent saying that there had been several additional offers on the business; however, the owner had decided that "spiritually" we were the right people to own the place, and he wanted to reopen negotiations.

He indicated that having the right people was more important than getting the right price. The other buyers had offered more than we had, but he was afraid they were going to develop the business in a way he found offensive. He had been a priest and had a deep appreciation for the serenity and spirituality of the place.

In fact, when his wife died he had a monument erected at what is called Prayer Rock. It was a place for meditation and reflection. He truly did want to be sure the unique character of this special place was not destroyed.

Joanne: So he had decided we were the chosen ones. We said, "That's all very nice, but we're still far apart financially." His agent said, "Well, he's interested in talking about some lease-to-own arrangement, and if you have any creative ideas of how we could work out a solution that would allow him to get close to what he's asking, that would be great."

Dom: So we started to think, "How can we do this?" We didn't have any down payment. This lease-to-own idea would give us an opportunity to get in with minimal risk and build some equity. If we could get the loan amount down and at the same time build the business, maybe it would work.

We proposed a yearly lease figure we felt the business could support to run three years, with the total amount to be applied to the purchase price. We offered a purchase price close to what he was asking. He felt he could go only two years and wanted a percentage that would not be applied to the purchase price, since he would be taking the business off the market.

And that's the deal we agreed upon. So we came up with a small amount of cash and prepared to take over the business.

Question: *As you look back at how you negotiated the deal, what did you learn?*

Dom: That if a deal is going to go, it works largely on the basis of trust. Over the years, I've negotiated many contracts. I've learned they are only as good as the people who enter into them. We worked hard on this deal to create a situation where both sides would feel good about the outcome. Trust was the important issue for the seller.

We also learned that everything takes twice as much time and work as we'd thought it would.

Question: *Is there anything you would change?*

Dom: We made one mistake. What we should have done was make the nonrecoverable amount we put in part of the purchase price. We should have increased the purchase price by that amount, because right now we're arguing with the bank about whether or not the cash we put in constitutes equity. The lesson is that any time you put money up, make sure it's going to be considered equity.

Question: *What was the experience like for you emotionally?*

Joanne: We pulled up every root we had. It was wrenching. Even though we were excited and we knew it was right, it was awful. We knew it would be painful. We didn't realize how painful. Half the time we were in ecstasy; the other half, in tears.

Leaving the area where we grew up, leaving family and friends, selling our home, starting over at middle age in a business we knew nothing about, leaving our careers—all of this was extremely traumatic.

We had agreed on the deal in November and planned to take over on March 1. There were a million details to settle in our personal lives and concerning the business. We had trouble paying attention to our jobs. We had to create the spring marketing brochure with no time to do it.

We were greenhorns and knew it. That added even more pressure. What had we missed because of our ignorance? What would come up that we hadn't foreseen? We were also embroiled in trying to sell my catering business at the same time. My staff was very angry and felt deserted by me.

Dom: It was very difficult for me to leave my company. I had been there since it began eleven years ago. I had difficulty concentrating. I was moody, absentminded. It was hard even to care anymore about things that were crucial to the operation.

Question: *You took over March 1, 1991. What were the first few months like?*

Joanne: One of the first things we talked about was how to allocate the responsibilities. My attorney said, "What are you two going to do? You've both run businesses. You're both headstrong. Now here you are, married, and about to run a business together. What are you going to do when you don't agree on what needs to be done or who needs to do it? You might want to think about a mediator."

We talked it over and decided we needed to resolve this issue. We delegated departments and budgets to each one of us. Each of us would be the ultimate authority when it came to his or her department.

Dom: We knew this could be a problem from talking with another couple who were innkeepers. In fact, they went into therapy to resolve the problem. They had a very difficult time until they stopped trying to run it like they ran their home and started to run it like a business.

It made all the difference in the world. They had weekly business meetings. Personal issues and business issues were now completely separated. Their world totally changed.

We took their advice. We had to deal with a lot of tough stuff. Meetings provided a necessary communication vehicle. The biggest thing was it provided a way to figure out who was responsible for what while we were operating in a situation where a lot of new things were surfacing that we didn't know about before.

Joanne: The first few months were interesting, to say the least. We were so green that we had to have the manger train us on how to take a booking. You'd think anyone would know how to do this, but it requires certain selling skills and tricks of the trade that you just wouldn't know.

We did a lot of maintenance that had been put off for years. The pipes froze just before we were due to open in April. Our first four groups of guests showed up after one o'clock in the morning.

I said to myself, "Holy mackerel, they were supposed to check in by two o'clock in the afternoon. It says so right here in the brochure. Is this what innkeeping is like?"

There were some management issues with the existing staff. We had new ideas about how we wanted things to be and tried to communicate our vision for Goose Cove Lodge in two key words: cleanliness and friendliness. Quality of food would become a major focus, along with clean rooms and better overall service. A number of the staff spent their time trying to keep things as they were. We didn't even think about resistance to change as an issue until we were confronted by it.

The best part was our guests. They were intelligent, well-heeled, sophisticated people. Most of them were very sensitive to the environment and appreciated nature, which is why they loved the place so much. They were searching for the peace and tranquillity that brought us to the place. We had little trouble relating to them.

Dom: We seemed to have one disaster after another. Shingles blew away, pipes froze, water heaters leaked, decks fell down, even an entire supporting wall in one of the cottages collapsed. We had infestations of carpenter ants. The engineer who had designed the septic system showed up and told us we needed additional work that we had not budgeted for. The electric company informed us that they had been drastically underbilling us for years and wanted thousands in back service charges.

Because of the economy we were taking a hit on our occupancy rate. The previous owner had been booked solid for most of the season. Several miracles occurred late in the season that saved us. We filled the place with a wedding and a photography convention.

Joanne: We also had a major movie being produced close by. The film company booked a block of rooms for eight weeks. So we were full, and, since it was late in the season, many of the staff had already left. What surprised us is that we operated effectively with half the staff. Boy, was there a lesson in that!

No question it was a tough opening, but in spite of all that, it was very satisfying. There is an aspect to Goose Cove that is very healing. That's why the guests keep coming back. The restorative rhythms of nature are very real. In one of the cottage journals, a couple had written, "We have found our souls here."

There were other surprises. Since the previous owner knew he would be selling the property, he didn't replace things like linens, bedspreads, or towels. There were also unexpected expenses in the kitchen. China, flatware, and napkins had to be replaced.

As new owners, we set quality goals, which required new and different standards. That required additional investment in new inventory. The other thing was if you have, say, 300 towels, is that enough? We were too inexperienced to know.

Question: *How is running the business different from what you thought it would be?*

Joanne: It's a tremendous invasion of privacy that we just didn't understand. It's sixteen hours a day, seven days a week during the season. We were drained by the middle of the season.

Dom: The sixteen hours a day is no exaggeration. You start at 5:30 A.M., and you're going until late at night. Everyone expects to meet and socialize with the innkeepers. There were always problems to solve that the staff couldn't handle.

I found myself having to do things I had not anticipated. At one point I even became a waiter. I'd never been a waiter. We were not eating properly. We were exhausted. It was a hectic six months.

Question: *Will it be any different this season?*

Joanne: Yes, we hope so. For one thing, I'll be out of the kitchen, spending more time on the desk and with the guests. We will also delegate more to a manager, freeing us up.

Question: *What are the benefits of running a business like this?*

Joanne: The physical surroundings are beautiful. The people are wonderful. We constantly meet and interact with fascinating people.

Dom: We get to enjoy what other people come here for in the summer, only we get to enjoy it for six months. It's truly a gift of six months. I don't want to paint a negative picture. Sure, there have been problems and it's been tough, but we have no regrets. We were emotionally ready for this.

Joanne: We're still on a steep learning curve. Once we learn what this is all about, we'll really enjoy it.

Dom: There are all sorts of legal, marketing, and management issues. Our backgrounds have proved valuable in dealing with them during the first year. That experience will really show in the second year.

Question: *Although you both feel you've made the right move buying this business, it wasn't easy. Any advice for others?*

Joanne: Yes, we've learned a lot. Other people may have different issues; however, there are probably lessons to be learned from our experience.

First, I think the fear of failure holds people back. As we've gained experience and years, we've outgrown our fear of failure. You learn that experience really does count and can be counted on. You'll learn as you go, and, even if things seem completely foreign to you, it's surprising how relevant past experience can pull you through.

I think most people finally learn that risk is a part of life. It's scary sometimes, but if you never take intelligent risks you probably won't accomplish much.

Dom: I agree. The hard part is actually deciding you are really going to do it. Then there is that moment of decision when you have to take advantage of an opportunity or it will pass you by. Be aware, recognize it when it comes, and seize it!

It's also important to persevere. There were times when we were very discouraged. Several times it seemed all was lost. But we hung in there, and here we are. There were parts of the negotiating process that were not fun. It was often frustrating that the seller didn't see it the way we saw it. But I think if you try to see the world through the eyes of the seller, your negotiating strategy will improve. You'll begin to understand what will work, so both sides will feel they've come out a winner.

As we strategized about how to buy this business, we realized that if it was going to happen, we had to convince the seller that we were the right people. We didn't really have much money to put in, so we had to be creative in other ways.

Joanne: I'd just like to say one final thing. Don't stay in an unhappy situation. Security is less important than happiness. If you really want to have your own business, make the decision and get on with it. Don't put it off until tomorrow, because tomorrow will never come. Besides, once you've made the change, you'll ask, "Why did I wait so long?"

16

Franchises

Case A: TV Facts
Case B: Grease Monkey

Case A: TV Facts

TV Facts is a publishing franchise. The franchisor supplies weekly TV listings and, as filler, short articles on the programs, somewhat along the lines of *TV Guide*. It's distributed free of charge to high-traffic retail outlets, such as supermarkets. Customers pick it up on the way in or out of the store. Supported solely by advertising revenue, the franchisee makes money by building a sales organization. Each week the franchisee assembles what is called "the book," consisting of a rough layout of the week's ads. It then goes to the printer.

Addie Tarbell began her career in social work writing and delivering training for social workers. She quickly became frustrated with the bureaucracy and work ethic.

> "Although I was making reasonable money, I was within four walls—not out where the action was. Because of the government red tape, it was difficult to make much happen. You couldn't work too hard because people would complain that you were making them look bad.

> "After a short stint in real estate and another running a small retail store in a seasonal resort town, I saw an advertisement for a business for sale. It turned out to be TV Facts. It was owned by a woman with two children and not enough time to run the business. I went out and talked with her and left with the financials.

"The franchise had been in business for eleven years. Originally it was bought and operated by a very good businesswoman, and she did very well. After getting married, she and her husband were involved in another business, so she sold it to a teacher. He had little interest, and the business did very poorly. After a short time he sold it to the woman I bought it from.

"She owned the business for a couple of years, and the business didn't do much better. When I went to see her, it looked pretty bleak. She did say that some of the revenue that would have shown was paid in merchandise, like refrigerators and furniture. And sure enough, she did have a bunch of stuff that looked as if it could validate that claim.

"My accountant was not impressed with the numbers. The owner wanted $25,000 for the company. There was no way he could make the numbers justify that figure. My lawyer was even less impressed with the franchise agreement. Believe it or not, it was sloppily typed in several different typefaces and poorly worded. He indicated that if this was an example of their level of professionalism, I should have reason to be concerned. So both my accountant and lawyer advised against buying the business.

"I decided to talk with other publishing franchisees to see what their experience was. The business concept was very interesting to me. It would get me out of an office and out on the road with customers. I found that extremely attractive. I reasoned that I should look at the business not so much in terms of what the current owner was able to do but what I was willing and able to do.

"So I talked with the head honcho of the franchise, and he gave me the names of other publishers. What they said confirmed my suspicions. If you took the business seriously and worked your tail off, you could do very well.

"Although my professional advisers said I should pay a price for the business based on what the business had actually done, I didn't agree. I made a decision to buy based on what I thought I could do. I had watched my mother run a similar publication in the real estate business with great success. Since this business operated in much the same way and I was a carbon copy of my mother, I had little doubt about my ultimate success.

"Another factor that convinced me to go ahead was the fact that I used the product every week and thought it was great. And most of all, I knew I'd love the actual work. I considered the sale price carefully. Although my accountant was technically correct—the business, based on past performance, certainly wasn't worth $25,000—it wasn't as bad as it might seem.

"The franchisor was selling new unworked franchises for $17,000. For a few thousand more I would be getting an established business with paying customers, distribution outlets, name recognition, and an eleven-year history. It seemed like a reasonable risk.

"It turned out that I was right. Although it was tough at first, the business was indeed out there, and revenues grew steadily. I worked a lot of hours. I saw every customer every week. After a year or so I was able to hire a salesperson, who helped accelerate the growth. Looking back, I have no regrets. It's been a wonderful experience.

"The interesting thing is, if I'd followed the direction of my lawyer and my accountant, I would never have bought it. It's certainly important to listen to them. Factor in their advice. But make the decision based on your own assessment. They tend to see all the warts and all the reasons not to buy. If it were up to accountants and lawyers, not many companies would get bought.

"I'll probably buy another business. The second time around, I'll be more diligent about checking out exactly what I'm buying. I got little support from the franchisor. I'll also spend a great deal of time asking hard questions of people who are experienced in the business. I'll want to know exactly why one succeeds or fails.

"The most important thing in evaluating any business opportunity is to assess whether your personality and background are a match. In my business, if I hadn't had a strong sales profile, forget it. And last, what is the market for the business like? Is it growing or declining? I want my success to be based on me, not on market conditions over which I have no control."

Case B: Grease Monkey

Grease Monkey International, based in Denver, Colorado, is a quick lube franchisor. It is the only company of this type not affiliated with a major oil company. It's the fourth largest franchise chain in the business. Started in 1978, the company has had a troubled past.

In 1991 Rex Utsler bought the controlling interest in the company and took over as president and CEO. A CPA by training, Rex has a broad management background, including starting and growing the highly successful Bountiful Corporation. Prior to that, he had been a corporate executive in the oil industry.

Question: *What motivated you to leave a comfortable executive position to own and manage your own business?*

Utsler: I guess I flunked vice president. I realized that if I were going to make a real difference, I had to have the authority to impact the outcome. Controlling your own business, you can do that.

And, fortunately, I had the opportunity to gain broad executive experience, which gave me the confidence to go it on my own. Financial reward is important to me. I could see that the only way to make serious money was to have a major interest in my own company.

Question: *What were you looking for?*

Utsler: I was looking for a business where I could obtain a significant ownership and assume the role of managing the company. After looking at a number of firms that required specialized knowledge, I realized that if I were to be successful in the role of CEO, I would have to limit my search to candidates that were low-tech or nontechnical. I was also looking for a company that was on the green side of the environmental issue. And since I came out of the service side of the oil business, I felt that my serious candidate would have to be a service company.

The other important thing I was looking for was a company that needed a change in management—something where my management experience could have a significant impact. I was not looking for a company that was well run and therefore maxed out in terms of taking advantage of good management techniques.

Question: *How did you find Grease Monkey?*

Utsler: I was introduced to Grease Monkey through a consultant who had been contracted to find someone who could raise some capital for the company. So I went in and took a look. Clearly they qualified on the environmental issue. Management was also very weak, so they qualified there. They were in bad shape, in fact probably close to bankruptcy, so they were seeking an infusion of capital.

Question: *So how did you proceed to investigate the opportunity?*

Utsler: Well, first of all I made it clear that I had no interest unless I could purchase the controlling interest. I spent a fair amount of time studing the financials and talking at length with key employees. I even leased a plane for eight days and flew around the country talking with franchisees. There were a number of them that were in noncompliance with their franchise agreements. That was very helpful in getting a handle on what the key problems were.

Question: *What are the major problems?*

Utsler: The problem was lack of management and lack of direction. The symptoms were a continuously deteriorating relationship with franchisees, resulting in an inability to collect royalties from existing franchisees and an inability to sell new franchises because of the poor reputation. They had also taken some bad leases on poor but expensive locations where they guaranteed the lease. That contributed to cash flow problems.

The other problem was that they were drifting without a plan to resolve the problems. They were in a downward spiral where the lack of cash caused a cutback on service to franchisees, and the lack of service resulted in a further decline in royalty income and further deterioration of the franchisee relationship.

Question: *With all that, you bought it?*

Utsler: That's why I bought it. In retrospect I underestimated what it would take to turn it around. We hadn't reached bottom yet with the franchisee relationship, and it took us longer than planned to get back on track. Certainly, the problems were serious. But I felt it had the elements of a good turnaround opportunity. The market was there and would continue to grow, and I saw the problems as management problems that could be solved. And because of the problems, I could buy in at an attractive price.

When I went out to visit the franchisees, I took the company's executives with me so they could also view the problems firsthand. They seemed receptive to the need for change. We could see that it would be a lot of work, but the company was very well positioned to grow and take advantage of new market opportunities. The industry was extremely fragmented, and I saw an opportunity to take advantage of that.

From a financial perspective, they had a negative cash flow of about $100,000 a month. It seemed to me that there were steps that could be taken that would stop that fairly quickly. Overall, I figured it would take about a year to arrest the slide and start moving things in the other direction. As it turned out, it was worse than I had seen, requiring me to draw on other capital to hold it together.

Question: *What are your feelings about the franchise concept?*

Utsler: Obviously, I believe in it. It's a very successful business model. Look at any strip mall and see who makes it and who doesn't. A good franchisor can take a lot of the risk out. But if you're going to consider a franchise, you must be a team player. You must be willing to accept a certain amount of regulation and be willing to give up some control. The franchisor can provide support services, name recognition, and clout with suppliers. The little guy benefits from economies of scale, ongoing research to develop new products, and highly effective advertising.

The important thing is that you have to be certain you're buying into a good franchise. With Grease Monkey, even though it had serious problems, I saw an opportunity.

Question: *So you bought the company. What was the plan? What did you do?*

Utsler: I made a few management changes. In addition to becoming chief executive officer and chief operating officer, I also assumed the post of chief financial officer so that I could get a handle on the financial issues as well as the overall management issues. Not having any prior experience in either the quick lube industry or franchising, I found it a challenge to get up to speed quickly so that I could make the right things happen.

Question: *What was that first year like?*

Utsler: Long. I underestimated the task, no question. But it's like owning a piece of art you like. The longer you own it, the more you see it and the more you like it. I found that to be true with Grease Monkey. I began to see even more growth opportunities than I was aware of at the outset.

A good deal of time was spent redesigning the accounting and financial reporting systems so that we could use the data to manage.

Question: *How did your employees and franchisees feel about your taking over the company with no experience either in franchising or in the industry?*

Utsler: There was a lot of apprehension. Everyone was aware that new vision was needed, and people were receptive to the idea that someone would make some firm decisions and go forward. I had a great reception from the franchisees who wanted the organization to survive and thrive.

I came in with a commitment to improve services to the franchisees in any way that I could and made it clear that my philosophy was that if you take care of the franchisees, they'll take care of the franchisor. This partnership concept had not been the cornerstone previously.

Question: *What was your plan for turning the company around?*

Utsler: There were two objectives: to eliminate any excuses for the franchisees not to pay royalties and fees—the commitment was to overdeliver on corporate services to them—and to set a precedent for aggressively enforcing the franchise agreement.

We worked out payment plans so that delinquent franchisees wouldn't feel hopelessly indebted and unable to pay. We worked out new supplier agreements. We made a commitment to add more staff to better serve our franchisees. And improving and developing staff became a priority. So the two objectives were to improve customer service to the franchisees and to improve the operational systems and process.

Question: *Were employees willing to go along with your plans, or did you encounter resistance?*

Utsler: There was a lot of resistance. They listened to me and then went back to doing things the way they always had. A number of people just wouldn't implement policy and procedure changes until absolutely mandated. In several cases, resistance resulted in personnel changes. It was extremely difficult.

Question: *If you could go back and begin again, what would you do differently?*

Utsler: The easier and quicker way would have been to change more of the personnel at the department head level. It's tough fighting old habits. The suggestions I had for change were consistently met with the attitude of "We already tried that and it didn't work." There was an unwillingness to admit that decisions that had been made in the past had been wrong. It would have been easier if I'd paid off the employment contracts and brought in a new management team. Although I would have lost some critical resources and the historical context, it still would have been easier to make the changes I considered important. I didn't do it because I felt vulnerable and had no contacts that would enable me to bring in the experienced people needed.

Another mistake I made was to underestimate the capital requirements. It would have been easier if I had a greater war chest. I spent a lot of time on aging receivables, but I didn't analyze the balance sheet as carefully as I should have. I wasn't aware of the magnitude of the accounts payable I was taking over.

Question: *How did you finally get people to come around?*

Utsler: After a while, people realized the changes were working. A change in attitude toward franchisees was causing them to have a much better attitude about the franchisor. But it has taken a long time, and there's still a way to go.

Question: *Buying a company that requires a turnaround is not for everyone. What advice do you have for people considering it?*

Utsler: First, make sure you understand exactly what the problems are. And I mean really understand them. Frequently there's more than meets the eye. Sure, it may seem attractive, but ask yourself, "If this is such a great deal, why am I so lucky?" Just as I did, most people underestimate what will be required to turn it around.

Second, once you understand the problems, do you have the skills to solve them? Usually the problems require broad management experience. If you're narrow, be careful. You've got to have a turnaround plan. You've got to know exactly how you're going to do it. It helps to have a good management team with you. It's almost impossible to do it alone.

You must be able to see where you're going to be in each of the next five years. And you must have thought through how you're going to get there. And then, do you have the capital, the talent, and so forth to take you there? It's especially important to have people around you who share your vision and who can take responsibility and action to make it all work.

Question: *You found your business through a personal contact. Any advice for others to help them identify prospective acquisitions?*

Utsler: Talk to everyone. Let people know you're in the market. Approach businesses that interest you. If they're not interested in selling, they may know someone who is. Ask people who have lots of contacts if they know of businesses that may be possibilities. Certainly accountants, lawyers, and bankers are all good people to ask. They often know of interesting situations.

I used several business brokers but had no success. They just didn't have the kind of businesses in their portfolio that would be of interest to me. You just have to keep looking. It will probably take a while to find it and a while to thoroughly investigate it and buy it.

Question: *You've been successful turning Grease Monkey around. If you had it to do over again, would you?*

Utsler: There have been times when I seriously doubted whether I'd made the right decision. It's been an emotional strain. But, yes, I would. It's very rewarding to see something succeed after all the hard work. We're now moving out, doing new things. We're developing franchises in Mexico, and that's very, very exciting.

17

Business Start-Up

The Lobster Company

This case, although technically a start-up rather than an existing company, has some valuable lessons for anyone buying a business.

Note particularly how the owners integrated life goals and career experience to develop the business concept and build it into their dream company complete with a life-style to match.

The Lobster Company

The Lobster Company is a food processing and distribution company headquartered on an island off the coast of Maine. The company is owned and operated by Ursula Kruse-Vaucienne and Stephen McCarthy, a husband-and-wife team. Steve, a lifelong New Yorker, and Ursula, a cosmopolitan European who has lived throughout the United States, are not what one would expect to find living in a rural fishing village literally at the end of the pipeline.

Ursula's business background is diverse, with experience in both government and big business. After completing a master's degree, she worked for a think tank at George Washington University and then spent several years working for the National Science Foundation. Her corporate experience includes stints in research and development, corporate planning, and sales and marketing.

Stephen has spent his career in the financial world. He has a bachelor of science degree in economics and a master's in finance. His experience includes pension work with insurance companies, and he holds licenses as a stockbroker and as a commodities trader.

Question: *Would you talk a little about your background?*

Ursula: I philosophically have divided my life into decades. First, I had my family very early. I considered my twenties the time to raise

221

my children. The thirties I viewed as a time to complete and refine my education. The forties I considered as the time to concentrate on making money. In my fifties I wanted to go into politics, and my sixties I wanted to devote to something like the Peace Corps or some other social service to give something back to society. And then in my seventies and beyond, I wanted to be involved in writing and lecturing to come back to my scholarly bent.

I did devote my twenties to raising my family, then moved on to university and government service, working with George Washington University and the National Science Foundation implementing international programs. These were chaired by Frank Press, who was the science adviser for President Carter. We worked with our Soviet counterparts to implement programs started by Brezhnev and Nixon in the early seventies.

I then moved on to the corporate world, where I worked for Honeywell for ten years. I started in the R&D center, learning about all kinds of technology transfer and innovation. I learned a great deal about how you introduce new ideas into the operating divisions. I developed a keen appreciation about how important it is to develop a constant stream of new ideas, regardless of the size of the company.

While in Honeywell corporate planning, I learned how to set up evaluation programs and how to analyze a new idea. I also worked for the semiconductor division, giving me good exposure to how a manufacturing organization works. I then had an opportunity to work extensively in the sales area. That ten years with Honeywell gave me a well-rounded education in every area of business, except for finance. I also never really cared for the financial side.

I was never interested in financial things until I met Stephen. We have a wonderful symbiotic relationship. He's strong where I'm weak.

Stephen: When I first met Ursula, she was known in the business as the cruise missile. She wasn't afraid to call on anyone. She has a wonderful ability, not only to sell people on her ideas, but to gain access to whomever she pleases.

Ursula: While working with the government, I had an opportunity to work with some of the best scientists in industrial research laboratories in both the United States and, to some extent, Europe. I also authored and coedited two books on Soviet science technology in the 1970s. As a result of my work at the National Science Foundation, I gained access to people at the highest levels. The result was a large network of contacts and friends who provide an incredible brain trust.

Question: *What is the value of all this experience?*

Ursula: By having exposure to so many different situations and people, I learned to be confident about what needed to be done in a business. I also learned that whether the business is big or small, the problems tend to be the same. And that exposure to R&D taught me that even what appears to be a big problem can be solved if a systematic problem-solving process is applied.

Question: *Stephen, how has your background prepared you for running this business?*

Stephen: I've spent a lot of my professional life raising money. And in raising money for others, you not only learn where the money is but also develop skills in evaluating the people and situations the money is being raised for. People tell me I'm a fairly good negotiator. And certainly, running a small business requires those skills. The Lobster Company has already presented a number of situations where negotiation experience has proved to be valuable.

I've always been more or less in business for myself because of the nature of the jobs I've held. I've always liked the idea of being paid commensurate with the success that I was able to generate, so I'm not uncomfortable with running a small business like this.

But, even though I love The Lobster Company, I would have never done it without Ursula. The only reason I'm able to shine is because she's backing me up with the critical material. She did the business plan for The Lobster Company. In the business world I'd be akin to a courtroom lawyer who is only as good as the people who put the case together. I don't have the head for putting together the required nuts and bolts that often spell the difference between success and disaster. I've never been a good detail person. I'm a good communicator, and that's part of the business, but someone had better be good at the detail work.

Question: *How did you decide to leave New York and move to Maine and get into this business?*

Ursula: We were not happy in New York; at least I wasn't. I just didn't want to continue living there. Stephen, being a wonderful partner, was supportive. So we were very open to looking elsewhere.

Stephen: We came to Maine because we saw an interesting house advertised. We were not seriously looking either to move or to look for a business opportunity at that point. We didn't like the house, but Ursula wanted to see Stonington, so we drove up.

Ursula: We do things on the spur of the moment. It was the Fourth of July weekend, 1991. The island was beautiful.

Stephen: By pure chance we met the person who was to become our business partner. It was late, and we asked someone where we could find a restaurant. We were directed to a small cafe called Rainbow's End. The name turned out to be prophetic. We got to the door and the fellow who owned the place said, "We're closed."

I said, "Well, we're really hungry." He said, "Well, come back in the morning and I'll give you breakfast." I guess I said to him, "That's easy for you to say, my friend. Your belly is full."

He laughed at that and said, "Come on in."

We got talking with him, and his daughter commented, "If my dad had some money, he could start a great company processing lobsters."

As the conversation developed, we asked him how much money he'd need and what he'd do.

Ursula: But it was only polite conversation. We were not in any way serious. We were not looking to start a company. And we were definitely not looking to go into the food business. We didn't even stay the night.

Stephen: About a month later we were sitting at home and decided to call him back. The idea had been just sort of percolating, I guess. We asked for more detail about the business he would start if he had the money.

Ursula: I took copious notes. The more information we had, the more I could see that there might be some interesting possibilities, at least enough to do some additional research. And since I was ready to do something else and I wanted out of New York, it was worth following up on.

Question: *What was it as you were talking with this fellow that got you interested? What was the business concept?*

Stephen: He said to us that you could take lobsters, which were plentiful, process and freeze them and build a very profitable business without a lot of expertise or money. If we could come in with about $150,000, we could rent the needed space. You could invest the money in lobsters, which is the inventory in this business, and you could then turn that inventory over fast. So your money wouldn't be invested in something that wouldn't be liquid.

Ursula: He said you'd need about $15,000 to invest in a rented facility and equipment. Everything else would be leased. He told us about the market, the processing, and the supply of raw material.

Stephen: We then thought through what a plan might look like. We decided to go up and take a look to see if what he said was true.

Ursula: This was outrageously different enough that, given Stephen's and my sense of adventure, we wanted to take a look.

Stephen: And there was a certain sense of romance about it too. Here you'd be in a New England fishing village right out of Norman Rockwell. You'd be dealing with fishermen. You'd be dealing with a product that has a certain romance attached to it. And it didn't require a lot of money or technical know-how.

Ursula: And most important, there was a strong market. We checked with several distributors who agreed that, if we could produce the product, they could sell it. We looked at the market carefully. We looked at the Canadian competition. We looked at the size of the market and what it would take to gain an adequate market share.

We talked to the state government, the university, the Food and Drug Administration, the U.S. Department of Agriculture, and the Department of Commerce. We asked about quality standards and the FDA Seal of Approval. We talked to many, many people, many organizations, including the lobstermen's organization. We did a lot of homework.

From that homework, we put together a business plan. We also took three trips to Stonington to verify our impressions. The downside risk seemed minimal.

Stephen: It looked right, and it felt right. And if it didn't work out, we wouldn't lose much.

Ursula: We were excited. We liked the people. We liked the work ethic we saw. We liked the frontier spirit. It was also summertime on the Maine coast, so we were there at a beautiful time of year. It was a new challenge, and we had nothing to lose. It was like having a baby together. I was convinced in both my heart and my mind that this was the right thing to do. We had looked at it carefully enough. The numbers looked right. The life-style looked right. We would not have made a move like this if the numbers weren't right.

Question: *What were the first few months like?*

Stephen: We moved in September. We rented an old captain's house with nine bedrooms. We were ready to get the business going and take advantage of the tail end of the season, which runs through November. But we couldn't negotiate a satisfactory lease with the owner of the pier where we were planning to open the plant. We had thought by October we'd have the necessary work done to open. So we put our money in a local bank and just took it easy for a while.

Ursula: Because we couldn't find the right space, the timing on our business plan was set back. We had planned to be operating in October 1991. We didn't open our doors until the fifteenth of May, 1992.

Stephen: Eventually we found a building and invested about $40,000 to upgrade it. We then found that it wasn't suitable because the sewage and water supply were inadequate. We couldn't have known that because we cut the deal in the dead of winter. We were led to believe that there would be no problems. So we processed for nine days, and then we walked. In the meantime, a local fishing pier came on the market, and, even though we hadn't intended to buy any property, we went ahead and made the commitment to buy it.

Ursula: There were a number of things that turned out to be much, much different from what we had anticipated. The biggest one was that we wanted to lease everything—not buy. That way we would have an easy way out without the obligation of heavy debt. Also, we wanted to conserve our resources.

Our original plan was to buy our lobsters at the public pier directly from the fishermen, but at a premium of forty to fifty cents per pound. When a private pier became available, we saw the opportunity to purchase our own buying station and save that premium price. Over time it would pay for the property.

Stephen: We're not afraid of problems. We operate on the premise that, as businesspeople, our job is to solve problems. When the pier became available, we acted quickly. We work well together as a team. Ursula has great people skills. People like her immediately. That's so important in getting people to do business with you.

We do move quickly when there's a problem or opportunity. We're not afraid to take a chance. We simply ask: What's the bottom line if it doesn't work out?

Ursula: So the plans changed. Instead of processing lobster as we'd planned, we became lobster dealers. We had the pier now. We bought lobsters at the pier and trucked them to Boston, making fifty cents a pound.

Stephen: We still needed a place to process lobsters. We learned that the local sardine factory was going to close. So we contacted the owner and started the negotiating process.

Ursula: It was exciting. Not scary, but we had many unanswered questions. We didn't know if it was available. We didn't know what it would cost. I had looked up the tax records and found that the tax base was $600,000. And for our purposes, a big building like that was not necessary. It was the largest building in town.

It also had an important history. At one time 150 people worked there. The sardine factory was the largest employer in town. We would only employ twenty-five to fifty people. We wondered if we were the right people to go after it. However, it was the only suitable facility. There just weren't any other places.

Stephen: It was a long negotiation process. We took over an existing lease with an option to buy. It took months longer than we had thought it would. We had thought we'd be up and running by the end of June. It was into the winter before the purchase was completed.

Ursula: Those were very heady times. Many times, one of us would get discouraged and say, "Do you really think we should do this?" We had serious doubts. Fortunately, we never had the doubts together. When one of us was low, the other was high. One of us always had the reasons and the will to press on.

Stephen: We decided to buy because it made sense as a real estate investment. The factory building was well built. It had the largest pier in town.

Ursula: We also worked with the Eastern Maine Development Corporation, a not-for-profit organization administering federal funds. They gave us a loan as part of the purchase price.

We also received training money from the government for our employees. Having been in government, I know it's fairly easy to locate funds. Either one of us alone would not have been able to pull this off. One and one is not two. It's eleven. Together we're able to accomplish so much more.

We've learned some important lessons. If we were doing it over again, we might look at things differently. We now know you can make money just selling lobsters live as a dealer. To make our profit projections in the processing side of the business, we need a critical mass of around 5,000 pounds a day. We'd like to process 10,000 pounds a day. The problem is that we sometimes were unable to get the 5,000 pounds we needed.

Stephen: This is our second year. We think we can get the lobsters we need this year. We're also looking at other ways of processing: processing whole, cryogenically freezing. We're working with the University of Maine on that. We have a lot of things in place now. We have all the facilities we need.

Ursula: We're also looking at introducing value-added products, such as stuffed lobster tails. There are so many exciting possibilities.

One of our big disappointments is that we had to let most of our employees go temporarily. We had hoped we could keep them for the winter.

We had thought we could process sea urchins. We tried it for three weeks, and it turned out to be a disaster. We ran into technical problems. We need to find someone who can teach us how to do it. We have the facilities, and we have the market. But in order to succeed we need to solve the processing problems.

Question: *How did you find the markets for your products?*

Ursula: We just call people up. We talk to just everybody who could get us to the right people.

Stephen: Our primary strength is marketing. We're not afraid to approach anyone if we see there is an opportunity to do business. Everyone is approachable. You just have to make up your mind that it's important and open up the line of communication. Not much is going to happen unless we're out there aggressively marketing The Lobster Company.

We sell through distributors and directly to people like Red Lobster and directly to other restaurants. We're planning to set up distributors in Florida, California, New York, and Washington.

Question: *As you look back at your first year, buying the facilities you needed and getting the business up and running and so on, what are your thoughts?*

Stephen: It's amazing how much time was spent just reacting to things that we had not anticipated. We've had to do some crisis mangement. But once we had made the decision to do this, there was no turning back. We just had to confront whatever problem came up, examine the alternatives, and work out a solution.

The company has grown into something bigger than we had envisioned. And it's been a lot more work than we had thought it would be. We've had to spend a lot of time on management issues. We've learned the ropes in dealing with the fishermen.

Ursula: We have surpassed our revenue goal for the first year by 50 percent. We've done okay in terms of profit, too. We have high payments on our real estate debt that we hadn't planned for. Even so, it's been a good year.

As much as I refined our business plan, everything cost more.

We way underestimated the expenses. And then we had the unanticipated expenses of moving the processing plant and buying real estate. All the while I thought we were estimating expenses fairly conservatively.

Fortunately, our revenue flow was better than forecast. The power of turning inventory over quickly has been a real help. Every time we turn inventory, we make money.

For the future, we have to create new products, get more out of the lobsters. Currently we throw 60 percent away. Research and development is a critical part of this business. My background will be valuable here. We've created a technical advisory board.

Question: *When people think about going into business or buying a business, fear is often a significant factor that holds them back. What kind of advice could you offer?*

Stephen: Ask what's the worst thing that can happen? How much money can you lose? What else might you lose? Can you live with that? Do you want to spend your life thinking you had a chance to do what you wanted and didn't take it?

Ursula: I think that, if you're too wedded to the security of the corporate world, you won't take that critical step that sets you free. When you're in your own business, you're it. There's no support to fall back on. If you think through what you are about to do and define certain parameters that you are to work within, a lot of the unknowns will disappear, and with them a lot of the fear.

You need to think through things like: What are you selling? What is your market? Where are you going to do it? How are you going to do it? What's the competition? And you must correctly anticipate cash requirements. Once you come to grips with these questions, you organize a detailed plan. Keep tight control on expenses.

At the same time, be open to new ideas. Be flexible and willing to modify your plan where it makes sense. If you can do these things, you have little to fear.

Stephen: There are many people who should not be running their own businesses. There's no place to hide. Failures can't be blamed on someone else. If you aren't comfortable with some personal risk, work for someone else.

Question: *What's it been like for you this first year? How has it been different from what you had anticipated?*

Ursula: We do everything from making financial decisions to shoveling bait.

Stephen: The nice thing about it is you're your own boss. But you're never away from it. It's your watch all the time. That's not a problem for us because we love it. You also learn to make decisions: bang! There's not time to do otherwise. Sure, you make some mistakes, but you just keep going. We've learned that none of this is life-and-death.

Question: *Having husbands and wives as business partners often turns out to be a mistake. What are the issues, and how do you cope?*

Ursula: Like all couples, we have our moments. But overall, it does work. First, we're older and have the luxury of experience. Each of us has also been successful in our own field. So there is not this feeling we have to compete to demonstrate our worth. We don't expect perfection. We accept each other's mistakes. When we have a problem, we bring it up and work it out constructively.

If we had done this when we were first married, I don't believe it would have worked. We have had time to develop a mature relationship. We know each other very well. We don't have the added problems associated with small children.

Stephen: You must truly be partners. You can't be the boss while your wife is the secretary or have the wife run the business while the husband is the maintenance person. Being partners is the only way it will work. If you don't feel the other person can pull his or her weight, you're likely to run into trouble.

I certainly wouldn't use getting into business as a way to save a marriage.

Ursula: The only way a partnership can work as a boss-subordinate situation is by agreeing that it is okay and clearly defining roles. Both must be truly comfortable with that. Most master-slave relationships don't work.

You must also recognize and respect the unique contribution each partner brings to the company. You must strive for consensus-based decisions, not win-lose, or else there will be great resentment. Ownership of ideas is not what is important. It's getting the best solution that is most important.

There's no way you can run a business together without conflict. It's how you manage it that's important. Be as considerate of each other as you would be of coworkers. It's not always easy, but no business disagreement is important enough to pay the price of permanently damaging your relationship.

Question: *What final advice do you have for people who are considering buying and running a small business?*

Stephen: There will be times when you'll feel like throwing in the towel. Maybe many times. But the secret is sticking with it; even when you know you're doing the right thing, it's often not easy. Perseverance is a characteristic of success in getting the business and running the business.

Ursula: Running a business requires constantly breaking new ground. Just because you haven't done it before doesn't mean you can't do it. As I grow older and accumulate experience, I realize that things aren't really that difficult. When you break a situation or task down into its components and then analyze each one of them, solutions will come and approaches will come. It's also a wonderful way to learn about yourself and a partner.

Finally, the most important thing in all of life is how you feel about yourself and your family. Being involved in running a company like this can be a lot of fun. But I know if I were not happy in my personal life, this could be really a drag.

18

Summing Up

A Final Checklist for Buying Your Business

If you've read this book from the beginning and you're still reading, congratulations. You've demonstrated a keen interest and a commitment to finding, buying, and operating your own business. If you're also under way with the exercises, you're way ahead.

Undoubtedly, you've concluded that a successful transition to the world of business ownership is a lot of work—a lot more than you had imagined. Then again, assuming you're no kid and have been around the block a few times, you know that any major life transition involves a lot of work. There are no shortcuts.

The good news is this process is highly effective "if used as directed." If you tough it out to the bitter end, you'll be delighted with the results. You'll uncover opportunities that won't surface in any other way. Ultimately, you'll unearth the situation that fits you like a glove. Others will call you lucky. You'll know better.

The Key Is Perseverance

Everyone who used this process has observed that it wasn't easy. In fact, most had thoughts of quitting. If you're typical, there will be times when you'll feel that you're just spinning your wheels. Then again, there will be times when you'll realize you've just made an important breakthrough.

Don't focus on either of those feelings. They simply don't mean much. Just when you think "Hey, this is a piece of cake!" you may plummet to the depths of despair. And just when you're ready to give up, suddenly things get much better and you resume the road to your goal.

The point is this: This process is no different than any other part of life. The inevitable ups and downs go with the territory. And the secret of success is the same. Successful people are no smarter than anyone else. They simply follow through regardless of the bumps along the way.

Cool Your Jets

Keep in mind that in the excitement of it all, it's easy to lose your bearings. Remember when you fell in love? Sure, there's nothing like it, but the condition certainly doesn't lend itself to cool objectivity. It is blind indeed.

Protect yourself by weighing carefully the input from trusted advisers. Your accountant and lawyer are a good start, but don't stop there. Select knowledgeable business associates you can trust to play the devil's advocate. Make them force you to justify your position.

Much of the research for this book was collected in interviews with people who were commenting on their personal experiences with the process. Although you'll make your own mistakes, there's no reason to repeat common errors. Let's conclude with a checklist of thoughts, ideas, and suggestions garnered from those who have blazed a trail for you.

Buyer's Checklist

1. Books like this are helpful, but they can take you only so far. Be certain that owning and managing your own business is right for you. The best way to know what you're getting into is to talk with people who've made the transition. If you've read the book, you know how to find them.

2. The process of buying your business should include the construction of a business plan. What do you intend to do with the business? The business plan will provide the road map for getting there and outline the financial investment and potential reward. That information may have a great deal to do with how you structure your offer to buy the business.

3. Be certain you understand the market. It won't matter how good you are if the market is changing in ways that may make your business obsolete. Pay particular attention to pricing and costs. If a competitive environment is squeezing prices, and the costs of doing business are escalating, watch out. Be especially wary of fad products and services that could be obsolete overnight.

4. Never, ever, buy a business without spending time with the customers. Without them, you have nothing. It's common for revenue to drop off significantly when a small business changes hands. Often a high percentage of the business is tied directly to the relationship between the owner and the customers. You must be able to gauge accurately how much of a problem that's likely to be. Otherwise, you may find that you've bought a start-up situation rather than an established business with a predictable cash flow.

5. Although you may have great ideas about where you can take the business, pay only for what it is—not what it might become. Would you pay twice as much for a rundown house because it has great potential?

6. Don't pay cash unless you can get a great bargain. Let the cash flow from the business pay for the purchase. Remember, the more paper the seller is holding, the more motivated she'll be to see you succeed.

7. Buying a business is like making a good soup. The deal should simmer for a while to bring out the best qualities. Since getting the best deal is often dependent upon the quality of the relationship between you and the seller, give it time. Neither personal nor business relationships develop their full potential overnight. Four to six months or more of fact-finding and negotiating is common.

8. Consider leasing the company for a year or two with an option to buy at prearranged terms and conditions. This would minimize your downside risk and give you a chance to see what you can actually do with the company. Sellers who are anxious to retire, who have a need to leave the business quickly for personal reasons, or who are having a difficult time selling the business are often willing to consider this option.

9. A company that is successful and growing will command top dollar. Consider buying a company in distress. They can be picked up at bargain prices. But be very careful. If you can't turn it around, it could get very expensive. Rather than, "I think I can turn it around," you must be able to say, "I know I can, and here's how."

10. The most difficult part of buying your business will be finding the right business to buy. Use every possible vehicle. Business opportunity ads, brokers, and the go-direct process described in this book. Contact bankers, lawyers, and accountants; they often know of companies that would profit from new ownership. Network with professional associates. Let them know you're in the market to buy.

11. Without exception, everyone interviewed for this book agreed, "I underestimated the financial demands of the business." Several advised, "Figure out what you'll need to run your company in the first year and double it." The same advice is true for time. It will take twice as long as you had planned to develop a new product, open new markets, find key employees, reach $5 million in sales, and so on.

12. You will also underestimate the resistance to change by the existing employees. It will take longer than you imagined and cost twice as much to get them aligned with your vision for the company. Remember that as you construct your offer to buy.

13. Always substantiate financial claims with tax returns. Financial statements for small, privately held companies are almost never audited. If the books are cooked, you could fry.

14. If you plan to grow the business, get commitments from vendors before buying. Be sure they will be able to meet your requirements at the right price. If necessary, identify secondary sources.

15. Be especially careful if you're buying a business in which you have no experience. Can you acquire the know-how easily and reasonably quickly? At the very least, spend a few days on the inside getting to understand the nitty-gritty of the business before you commit.

16. If you're planning to involve your spouse or some other partner in the company, make sure the goals are shared. Discuss and agree on roles and responsibilities. Determine how disputes will be resolved. Define how you will separate business and personal life.

17. Don't bet the entire farm on your new venture. Decide what you can afford to lose and still live with the consequences. Families have been destroyed because the money they borrowed from relatives was lost. Think how you'd feel about losing your parent's life savings.

18. Terms are as important as the sale price. Remember the Rule of One-Third. After a down payment of one-third, the cash flow must provide your salary, a return on your down payment, and the money to service your debt. If the business is not generating enough cash to do that, lower the price, modify the terms, or both.

19. When negotiating the deal, don't listen to what the seller says, listen to what he means. For instance, the seller may say, "I can't take less than a million." Translation: "I'm worried I'll run out of money during retirement." Or the seller may say: "I want all cash, no terms." Translation: "I'm afraid you'll run the business into the

ground and I'll have to come back and save it." Get beyond the symptom of the problem (what the seller says) to the root cause of the problem (what the seller means). Then, together you can find a solution that makes you both smile.

20. Don't lose sight of why you're buying a business. You wouldn't leave your current job for a high-paying job you would hate, so don't buy a business you can't get excited about simply because it's a great deal. Few people succeed in a business they find dull and boring.

Finally, like all great accomplishments in life, finding the company that's just right for you will take time. One to two years isn't unusual. However, taking whatever time is required will pay off both in dollars and in establishing a great way to make your living. But there's more. Owning and running your own business is a statement of philosophy and life-style.

If you've decided that owning your own business is where you should be, don't settle for anything less. Do what makes you happy. You hold in your hands the way to make it happen. Best wishes and happy hunting.

Index